Troublemakers

Troublemakers

LESSONS IN FREEDOM FROM YOUNG CHILDREN AT SCHOOL

Carla Shalaby

THE NEW PRESS

25 YEARS

NEW YORK
LONDON

Requests for permission to reproduce selections from this book
should be mailed to: Permissions Department, The New Press,
120 Wall Street, 31st floor, New York, NY 10005.

The Publisher is grateful for permission to reprint the following copyrighted material:

"(Something Inside) So Strong" Words and Music by Labi Siffre. Copyright
© 1987 XAVIER MUSIC LIMITED. All Rights in the United States and
Canada Controlled and Administered by UNIVERSAL - POLYGRAM
INTERNATIONAL PUBLISHING, INC. All Rights Reserved Used
by Permission. Reprinted by Permission of Hal Leonard LLC

"Caged Bird" from *Shaker, Why Don't You Sing?* by Maya Angelou, copyright
© 1983 by Maya Angelou. Used by permission of Random House, an imprint
and division of Penguin Random House LLC. All rights reserved.

Images and text from *Don't Let the Pigeon Drive the Bus!*, words and
pictures by Mo Willems. Text and illustrations copyright © 2003 by
Mo Willems. Reprinted by permission of Disney • Hyperion Books,
an imprint of Disney Book Group, LLC. All rights reserved.

Image from *Don't Pigeonhole Me!* by Mo Willems. Copyright
© 2013 by Mo Willems. Reprinted by permission of Disney Editions,
an imprint of Disney Book Group, LLC. All rights reserved.

Published in the United States by The New Press, New York, 2017
Distributed by Two Rivers Distribution

ISBN 978-1-62097-236-6 (hc)
ISBN 978-1-62097-237-3 (e-book)

CIP data is available

The New Press publishes books that promote and enrich public discussion and
understanding of the issues vital to our democracy and to a more equitable world.
These books are made possible by the enthusiasm of our readers; the support
of a committed group of donors, large and small; the collaboration of our many
partners in the independent media and the not-for-profit sector; booksellers, who
often hand-sell New Press books; librarians; and above all by our authors.

www.thenewpress.com

Composition by dix!
This book was set in Fairfield LH

Printed in the United States of America

14   15   16   17   18   19   20   21

For Akenna, Izaac, Izaiah, Jordan, Sophia & Trevor—
You are the young people from whom I learn love;
may you forever continue your teaching.

100% of royalties from *Troublemakers* will go to the Education for Liberation Network, a national coalition of young people, teachers, community activists, parents, and researchers who imagine and enact education as the practice of freedom.

Contents

Foreword   xi

Preface: Canaries in the Mine   xv

Introduction: On (In)Visibility   xxv

Part One: Forest School   1

Zora: On Being Out-Standing   9

Lucas: On Being Pigeonholed   41

Part Two: The Crossroads School   73

Sean: On Being Willful   83

Marcus: On Being Good   115

Conclusion: Trouble-Making in School   151

A Letter to Teachers: On Teaching Love and
   Learning Freedom   171

A Note to All Readers: On Mushrooms, Mold, and Mice   183

Acknowledgments   189

Suggested Resources   195

Notes   201

Foreword

We rarely hear the words *freedom* and *love* in our private conversations and public discourses on schooling, in our aspirations and hopes for our children's education, in our proposals and recommendations for school reform. In fact, these concepts—embedded in theoretical propositions, in moral searching, or in empirical investigations—are rarely on the tongues of educational researchers who examine the dynamics of teaching, trace the trajectories of child development, and explore the layers of school culture. In this educational era, resonating with appeals for standards and standardization, driven by the requirements of accountability and evaluation, the words, metaphors, and images that come to our minds and haunt our public consciousness carry just the opposite meaning: they speak of uniformity and conformity, management and control, of achievement and success as measured by narrow assessment tools and remote, quantifiable metrics. They tend to be blind to, and mute about, those powerful dimensions of classroom life that are shaped through intimate relationships, through community building, through honoring the rich variations and differences among us. They do not recognize or appreciate that education is a complex human enterprise requiring creativity and imagination, heart, mind, and soul, struggle and suffering, grit and grace. In our efforts to control and measure, in fact, we often confuse difference with deviance, illness with identity; we pathologize, exclude, and then label those children who do not fit the norm—who trouble the waters, who misbehave—and we reward the teachers who contain and squelch the troublemakers.

In this beautiful and provocative book—incisively argued and artfully composed—Carla Shalaby puts the ideas and ideals, the concepts and the practices, of freedom and love front and center. She does not offer up sentimental soliloquies on love or ideologically inspired rhetorical riffs on freedom. Rather she speaks about "teaching love and learning freedom" as deeply relational, respectful endeavors that must be threaded into the fabric of a humanistic education. She is referring to the kind of love that she believes should permeate every relationship between teacher and student; a love of symmetry and devotion; a love that is tough and demanding, but also enduring and forgiving; a love that makes the other person feel seen and worthy. Shalaby believes that the language and culture of love should be a part of scholarly discourses about education: love and advocacy should shine through teachers' relationships with their students and love should be at the center of community building and belonging in school classrooms. She also sees classrooms as places where we must practice freedom; places where children must be treated with reverence and dignity as free persons; "microcosms of the kind of authentic democracy we have yet to enact outside those walls"; spaces for children to lift up their voices—individually and collectively, in harmony and cacophony—and say what they need and who they are.

Troublemakers is in many ways an exploration of the ways in which schools are too often institutions of separation, erasure, and exclusion, not love and freedom. Shalaby draws deep and penetrating portraits of four children who have been identified by their teachers as troublemakers; her inquiry rests on the conceit that in carefully examining the perspective and experiences of these children—as they navigate their classroom and home environments and as they build their relationships with their teachers and peers—we will learn something significant about how the cultural and structural arrangements of school may be inhospitable for all—or most—children. Shalaby brings to the writing her signature blend of provocation, inspiration, and insight, her clear-sighted empathy and advocacy for the children. Combining portraiture, person-centered ethnography, and visual-arts methods—which allow her to see, see with, and draw the children—she is an attentive listener, discerning observer, intensely curious questioner, and occasionally a playful co-conspirator. She is witness, friend, advocate, and analyst, moving across these roles with alacrity.

Even as she keeps the children in view and documents their provocations and disruptions, the drama and troublemaking they stir up, and their perspectives, voices, and reasoning, she also offers a fair and knowing portrayal of their teachers. There is no blame game here, as Shalaby closely examines the motivations, intentions, strategies, and relationship-building of teachers, and recognizes the ways in which they too get tangled in the web of norms, rules, and requirements of the institution; the ways in which they often see, and can name, the compromises, dualities, and contradictions that confront them each day even while they feel helpless in resolving the tensions productively; the ways in which they are good people trying to raise good students in a way that sometimes feels joyless and sad, difficult and demeaning.

The troublemakers are the caged canaries, children who are more sensitive than their peers to the toxic environment of the classroom that limits their freedom, clips their wings, and mutes their voices. The canaries' songs warn us of the dangers—dangers to children's learning and development, to their self-worth, to their physical health and emotional well-being—as the misbehaving children struggle for visibility and voice in an institution that works to ensure their invisibility; as they work to be embraced by their classroom communities but behave in such a way that will ensure their exclusion; as they seek interdependence in a setting where the norms of independence prevail; as they raise their voices louder and louder hoping to be heard, but know they will be silenced.

Shalaby recognizes that seeing schools as primary sites for teaching love and learning freedom is countercultural, even revolutionary, and oppositional to the ways that schools are traditionally organized, contrary to the ways teachers are trained, evaluated, and rewarded, counter to the ways our society perceives and places value on children. It requires a radical reframing of the values and goals embedded in definitions of achievement and success in schools, a recasting of classroom rules, rituals, and pedagogies, a redrawing of the boundaries of community, and a reshaping of the hierarchies of power and authority in schools. Shalaby knows, and warns us, that the work of transforming our schools is hard and beautiful, tough and generous. It is filled with minefields and misunderstandings, breakthroughs and revelations. The work is one of re-imagining what a free and loving learning place might be, and children are the best source for beginning this envisioning and liberating project. They are, after all, the great imaginers: they will lead the way, the troublemakers at the front of the line. We must begin by listening to them.

Sara Lawrence-Lightfoot
Emily Hargroves Fisher Professor of Education
Harvard University

Preface

Canaries in the Mine

The more you refuse to hear my voice, the louder I will sing.
—Lyrics from *Something Inside So Strong* by Labi Siffre
Sung by children in Freedom Schools across the country

The pages of this book are devoted to the experiences of four young children at school. I care about the lives of children at school because I am an educator, and as an educator it is my job to insist on every child's right to a classroom experience that daily honors her, reveres her smarts, engages her curiosities, and ensures her dignity.

But I also care about the lives of children at school because I am a human being, and as a human being I recognize every child's unalienable right to be free. When I speak of a child's right to freedom, I mean that by virtue of being human she is endowed with the unassailable right *not* to have any part of her personhood assaulted or stolen. A free person can expect to be seen and treated as a full human being, free from any threats to her identity, to her cultural values and know-how, to her safety and health, and to her language and land. A free person retains her power, her right to self-determination, her opportunity to flourish, her ability to love and to be loved, and her capacity for hope.

A free person recognizes when she or others are being treated as less than fully human. And a free person embraces both her right and her duty to struggle against such treatment and to organize with others to do the same as a solidary community. This book is informed by this essential definition of every young person's right to be free, and by my belief that education is one of the primary means to realizing this freedom.

As an educator and a human being, then, I understand school to be not only a place where young people must be treated as free persons but—more important—a place where they can learn, together, how to skillfully insist on their right to be treated as free people. Classrooms must be places in which we practice freedom. They must be microcosms of the kind of authentic democracy we have yet to enact outside those walls—spaces for young people, by young people—engaging our youth to practice their power and to master the skills required by freedom.

By and large these are not the schools we have now. For the most part, schools value quiet children over loud ones and operate as though adults are the only teachers in the room. The adults get to speak while the young people listen. Questions are answered rather than asked. Our schools are designed to prepare children to take their assumed place in the social order rather than to question and challenge that order. Because we train youth in the image of capitalism instead of a vision of freedom—for lives as individual workers rather than solidary human beings—young people are taught academic content that can be drilled and tested rather than understanding literacies and numeracies as forms of power, tools for organizing, fodder for the development of their own original ideas.

Even our supposedly "best" schools—maybe especially these most well-resourced, largely white schools—fail to give young people a chance to teach and learn the meaning, the responsibilities, and the demands of freedom. Schools serving the wealthy do the most extraordinary job teaching children to define success in

individual rather than collective terms—to get ahead rather than
to struggle alongside, to step on rather than to lift up. On any serious measure of practicing freedom, these would be the "failing"
schools.

We pay dearly for our failure to teach freedom, for our refusal to
insist on being fully human, and for our selection of just a precious
few who are granted the right to matter. Our children bear witness
to an unimaginable array of examples of throwaway lives: mass
shootings in nightclubs, on college campuses, and in elementary
schools; bombings in stadiums and cafes, during city marathons,
and on trains; countless communities dislocated and eradicated by
war, gentrification, and other land grabs.

Though often perpetrated by individuals, such violence thrives as
a reflection of and in response to institutional and state-sanctioned
violence—historic and ongoing genocide and terror; criminalization and mass incarceration; segregation and poverty; patriarchy,
homophobia, and sexual violence; colonization and imperialism;
xenophobia, racism, and the enduring supremacy of whiteness.
These interconnected machineries of violence are built into the
foundation of our nation, and our children saw them given new life
and strength when we recently elected a president who explicitly
promoted them, celebrated them, and promised to maintain them.

What is the role of education in the lives of children carrying the
burden of this witness, breathing these poisons into their delicate
lungs?

The images of violence reside in their imaginations, teaching
them lessons in throwaway lives and crowding out more beautiful,
more human possibilities. Some see the images on television, at a
distance. Others live it up close, day to day: taking longer routes to
school to avoid the deadliest corners of their neighborhoods; losing their fathers, brothers, and friends to prisons designed for and
profiting from their confinement; being evicted from their homes
and having their water shut off or poisoned; enduring the fear of

having their parents deported while they work impossible hours for unlivable wages; being murdered by officers of the state hired to protect them.

Our children are learning that only some lives matter, that only some deaths are tragic, that only a precious few deserve relief from suffering. We need schools that offer young people a chance to grapple with these lessons—schools fueled by the imperative to imagine and to create a world in which there are no throwaway lives. Any of us invested in the rights of persons to be free have cause to care about the lives of children at school and to resurrect our imagination for schooling as a deeply human, wildly revolutionary site of possibility.

I am calling on all educators—those in our classrooms, in our homes, and on our streets—to embrace and to respond to the urgency of our collective need to teach love and to learn freedom.

Children—especially the youngest of children—are masters of imagination. When I am burdened by the heavy weight of reality, soul-weary and stuck, young children are able to inspire my imagination for a more playful, more creative way forward. Because designing classrooms in the image of freedom requires an extraordinary degree of imagination, I enlisted the four young children featured in this book—whom I call Zora, Lucas, Sean, and Marcus, to protect their anonymity—to light our path toward a new vision. I will forever be grateful to these six- and seven-year-old teachers. I learned so much from them about how to be truly human, what we are each entitled to just by virtue of being human, and how hard some people must work to be recognized as fully human in everyday life.

I chose these four children carefully. In school we generally identify the most pleasant, most compliant children as our leaders. But if being a leader means doing exactly as one is told, we should wonder what it means to be a follower. I have chosen differently. I asked teachers to identify the children presenting the most challenging behaviors in their classrooms. Interested in freedom, I needed the children who sing the most loudly rather than those who follow orders for quiet. These are the children who do not always cooperate, who cannot or will not comply with the demands of their teachers. They are the children who make trouble at school—the troublemakers. They have been my teachers and, in these pages, they will become yours.

In my countless visits to classrooms over the last decade, I have witnessed these troublemaking children being punished with regularity—reprimanded, detained, isolated, removed. They are not described as leaders, as children from whom we might learn. Instead, the descriptions are invariably disparaging: angry, damaged, disturbed, out of control, impossible. Justifications for their daily mistreatment are made on the basis of their own alleged bad behavior, as if they themselves have chosen to be treated as less than fully human in school. Thus, they are held personally accountable for the assaults to their personhood that they endure daily in our schools.

Routinely pathologized through testing, labels, and often hastily prescribed medications, these young people are systematically marginalized and excluded through the use of segregated remediation, detentions, suspensions, and expulsions. The patterns of their experiences, especially those of older children, are well documented in what we know about the school-to-prison pipeline. But this pipeline begins disturbingly early. Children as young as two years old are expelled from their preschools at an alarming rate—a rate, in fact, that is more than three times higher than the national K–12 expulsion rate, disproportionately impacting children of color to a degree that should sound civil rights alarms. According to the most recent data from the U.S. Department of Education, black preschoolers are 3.8 times more likely to be suspended than their white peers.[1] These little ones are deemed problem people before they even begin kindergarten.

These troublemakers—rejected and criminalized—are the children from whom we can learn the most about freedom. They make noise when others are silent. They stand up against every school effort to force conformity. They insist on their own way instead of the school's way. These young people demand their freedom even as they are simultaneously the most stringently controlled, surveilled, confined, and policed in our schools. They exercise their power despite being treated as if they have none.

Criminalizing troublemakers is our historic, cultural routine. Folks who demand the rights of people to be free—Mahatma Gandhi, Assata Shakur, Nelson Mandela, Harriet Tubman, Dr. Martin Luther King Jr., Angela Davis, to name just a few—are regularly detained, jailed, and systematically harassed by officers of the state. This habit persists. We witness protestors in Ferguson teargassed, high school students in Baltimore handcuffed and loaded into paddy wagons while demanding school reform on the steps of their city hall. Jasmine Richards, a Black Lives Matter activist, was convicted for "felony lynching," jailed because she tried to pull a woman away from the police. Acts of disobedience, even in the name of justice, are punished. Thus, on our streets and in our schools, we are in the habit of incarcerating the people from whom we could learn the most about freedom. We cage the birds singing most loudly.

Zora, Lucas, Sean, and Marcus call out the need for us to listen to their strained freedom songs. If we learn to hear them, we can build our own capacity for refusal and our own imagination for schools, and for a world, in which there are no throwaway lives.

Though this book centers on the rights of free persons to be recognized as fully human, I begin here with some talk of animals—animal sentinels, in particular. Animal sentinels are species purposefully used to provide advanced warning of disease, toxins, and other environmental threats to human lives. They are selected

based on their heightened susceptibilities to particular hazards—
the more sensitive they are to the poison, the better—and they
are often sacrificed to save us. Bats are used to measure pesticide
contamination, mollusks for assessing water quality; honeybees tell
us about air pollution. They suffer so we don't have to.

The classic example of an animal sentinel is the domestic canary, used in the early twentieth century to alert miners of deadly
carbon monoxide in the coal mines. The miners brought these
caged canaries with them into the mines. Because the birds are
small and have particularly sensitive respiratory systems, the poison kills them more quickly than it would a human being, leaving
the coal miners enough time to save themselves. I remember learning about the miners' canary, shaken by the images of these starkly
bright yellow birds, tiny, fragile, beautiful—caged in the dirt and
the lightlessness of those mines.

I think of the children who make trouble at school as miners' canaries. I want us to imagine their behaviors—which are admittedly
disruptive, hypervisible, and problematic—as both the loud sound
of their suffering and a signal cry to the rest of us that there is poison in our shared air. That is, when a child is singing loudly—and
sometimes more and more loudly, despite our requests for silence—
we might hear that song as a signal that someone is refusing to hear
her voice. And we might learn to listen, heeding her warning and
searching our air for the toxin triggering her suffering, the harm
that simultaneously silences her and forces her to scream out.

Of course, we typically respond to troublemaking by holding children themselves solely accountable for transgressions, searching
for problems with their minds or bodies, punishing them through
time-outs and detentions that graduate to more consequential
forms of exclusion over time, and too often medicating them into
docility. When I visit classrooms, it is not at all unusual to see children as young as five made to sit apart from all the other children
for weeks at a time, sent out into the hallway as punishment even

during instructional time, or required to sit with their faces to the wall. Isolation, humiliation, and exclusion are commonplace school responses to misbehavior, and these responses happen with such frequency in all kinds of schools that they are considered acceptable and seen as inevitable.

Teacher preparation programs around the country train new teachers to believe that these less-than-human responses are strategies of good classroom management. These often idealistic and earnest teachers-to-be are taught that good teachers command control over students, and they are encouraged to learn to use behavioral systems of reward and punishment that are actually more appropriate for training animals than for educating free human beings.

Teachers-in-training learn to punish transgressions because it is not controversial to be castigated if you misbehave. It is your choice and your fault. This logic is deeply embedded in the American psyche—the nation with one of the highest incarceration rates in the world—and it justifies our decision to throw away young lives by making young people think the fault for that exclusion is entirely their own. It seems impossible to blame a caged bird for its own death in a toxic mine, but we nonetheless manage to do so.

Thinking of these troublemaking children as canaries in the mine is not my own idea. I learned it from Thomas, the father of a five-year-old boy who could not and would not comply with the behavioral expectations of his kindergarten teacher.[2] Teachers, school administrators, medical doctors, and psychologists all searched for pathology in the mind and body of this child. Their assumption was that the arrangements of school were normal and good, so any child unable to tolerate those arrangements had to be abnormal and bad.

Though the child suffered from a mood disorder, a diagnosable brain illness, Thomas challenged the assumption that the disease made his son inherently broken or bad. Much like the canary's fragile lungs, this child's brain leaves him more susceptible to the harms of poison. He's more sensitive to harm than the average child. Still, the problem is the poison—not the living thing struggling to survive despite breathing it. After all, in clean air, canaries breathe easily.

With this perspective, Thomas drew attention away from his son and instead toward the toxic air of life in schools—the daily harms that less susceptible children can breathe in more readily: being told what to do and exactly how to do it all day; the requirement to sit still for hours on end; the frustration of boring, disconnected, and irrelevant academic tasks; shockingly little time for free play; and few opportunities to build meaningful relationships in community with other children and loving adults. These were the daily realities his son complained about, reacted to in the extreme, and refused to tolerate. Yet they are all too common in the life of schools, invisible because of their everyday normalcy. Thomas's son made them visible, signaling their danger with his hypersensitive reactions to the harm. He was a miner's canary, warning us all about threats to freedom that we might not otherwise see.

Understanding supposedly broken children as miners' canaries focuses our attention on the toxic social and cultural conditions of schools that threaten and imperil the hope of freedom. Our work as educators and as parents must become an effort to clean our air instead of condemning young people, forcing them and actively training them to tolerate the poison.

Maya Angelou wrote of the caged bird in her well-known poem of that name:

> *But a bird that stalks*
> *down his narrow cage*
> *can seldom see through*
> *his bars of rage*

his wings are clipped and
his feet are tied
so he opens his throat to sing.

I invite readers to listen carefully to the strained songs of the four young children whose experiences are captured in this book; to understand challenging behavior as the result of clipped wings, tied feet, and the rage that people naturally and understandably experience when their freedom to live as full human beings is limited to the confines of cages.

The caged bird sings
with fearful trill
of the things unknown
but longed for still
and his tune is heard
on the distant hill
for the caged bird
sings of freedom.

Introduction

On (In)Visibility

In my first year as a teacher, I was lucky enough to meet Anthony. At nine years old, Anthony stood taller than me and knew more about many subjects—dinosaurs, technology, astronomy—than I would ever know. He loved the freedom of learning just enough to hate the constraints of schooling, and he did what I asked only if it happened to coincide with what he wanted to do. His behaviors daunted me as a novice teacher and would likely still challenge me today: talking over his classmates, being physically aggressive on the playground, destroying classroom items, ignoring my directives, walking out of the room. I woke up in the morning anxious about the day with him and went to bed worn out by him. I barely remember whom else I taught in those 180 days; Anthony had made himself both visible and memorable.

At the time, I was a twenty-two-year-old fresh out of teacher training, and I somehow felt that the combination of my credentials and my status as an adult should signal to Anthony my clear authority over him—my earned, legitimate right to control his activities and his behavior. I was in charge of asking the questions and he was charged with answering them. I was the adult, the teacher, the leader. He was the child, the pupil, the follower. We were in a school. All of these facts added up to a clear and singular conclusion: I had power over him, and his success relied on his ability and willingness to accept that. I didn't much question these roles and expectations because they are normalized in teacher preparation programs and in the everyday life of classrooms, part and parcel of the seemingly natural order of things in school.

Lately, though, as I spend considerably more time with growing babies and toddlers, the demands of school seem increasingly antithetical to how children *be* in the world. With these youngest of people, the desire for self-directed learning is fierce. They move and run and jump and skip; they do not sit still for long stretches. They learn to do new things—crawl, talk, walk—when they are ready, not when adults decide they should be ready. And though dependent on caretakers, young children eagerly seek and exercise autonomy. They tirelessly refuse, protest, and question. *No* and *why* are the favored words of little ones.

School does not welcome this protest, this natural way of childhood. As soon as they cross the threshold of a school building, increasingly under the gaze of surveillance cameras, police officers, and metal detectors in our city schools, they are expected to know a lot about social control and to accept the fact of it. Everyone is at the ready to catch children doing the wrong thing. Unquestioning deference to authority is the requirement and the expectation of school, where adult directives replace children's own desires.

Kids learn the culture of school quickly. In a second-grade classroom I visited, children were tasked with drawing illustrations to accompany newly acquired vocabulary. For the word *obedience*, where I expected a picture of a dog, perhaps, I instead found a young artist who had drawn a row of pupils at their desks sitting straight, hands clasped, facing forward. It was a haunting image and, also, a deeply resonant one.

Some elementary school teachers have proudly managed to hold on to "choice time," a brief moment for free choice and play in an otherwise packed day of formal academic instruction. Still, the very fact of choice time reveals that the rest of school time *lacks* choice. The relative fun of the preschool years is replaced by the rigidities and demands of formal, comprehensive, compulsory schooling. As Philip Jackson, a researcher of schools, long ago reminded us, there are only three institutions from which Americans are allowed no escape: prisons, mental hospitals, and schools.[3]

Unsurprisingly, then, kindergarten teachers note many "problems" in children's transition to school. In one study, researchers found that as many as 46 percent of kindergarten teachers report that more than half their class has trouble following directions; 34 percent report that children struggle to work independently; 20 percent report that their kindergartners have poor social skills and are "immature."[4] These figures ought to lead us to question whether the demands of early schooling are reasonable; after all, it seems we should expect immaturity from a five-year-old. If nearly half of our children fail to follow directions, we should question the appropriateness of the requirement.

Instead, we turn a gaze of pathology on children. At the age of five, if you cannot follow directions and work independently, you are likely to begin a long series of interactions with the school's various mechanisms for identifying, labeling, and remediating deficits. Suddenly and swiftly, children become problems.

Any teacher, in any type of school, can readily and immediately name these "problem children." Young people who prove unwilling or unable to comply are necessarily problematic and easily identifiable. And despite decades of research on classroom management and discipline—undertaken by psychologists, sociologists, educators, anthropologists, criminologists—so-called bad behavior persists and so does teachers' nearly universal exasperation with it.

Elementary school teachers, especially in urban centers, name behavioral challenges as their number one issue of concern, often identifying disruptive behavior as the biggest issue facing their schools. Up to 50 percent of novice teachers who leave the profession in their first five years cite student behavior as their foremost reason.[5] Anyone interested in the effectiveness and success of teachers, and in their willingness and ability to stay in the profession over the long haul, has reason to care deeply about student behavior.

Those invested in the success and general well-being of children, too, have reason to take interest in how our young people are disciplined in schools. We have known for decades that children who feel themselves to be academically lagging will more often engage in problematic behaviors. Yet, if this is the chicken, there is also an egg; young people who misbehave are often punished by exclusion, therefore missing academic content and falling further behind. "Zero tolerance" policies reign supreme, imposing immediate and automatic punishments for lapses in student conduct, while the use of suspension and expulsion is reaching epidemic proportions despite their well-documented ineffectiveness in curbing incidences of misconduct. Young people are forced to miss school, even as they are simultaneously punished for being late to or absent from school.

Even in schools that do not rely heavily on out-of-school suspension and expulsion, other forms of exclusion dominate the response to noncompliance: time-outs, being sent to the principal's office, in-school detention and suspension, time away from class to work with counselors, social workers, and psychologists, "break" areas that are most often placed apart from the instructional area of the classroom. These are all responses that hinder children's access to academic content and that also threaten their sense of belonging and their ability to contribute to the community of their classrooms.

Students who do not behave by our standards are then not permitted to progress by our standards. Many cases of dropout are actually cases of *pushout*, in which students are suspended and expelled so often that moving forward in school becomes impossible. Missing out on school, especially in the early grades, when the most formative and basic skills are supposed to be taught, has severe and lasting consequences on a young person's persistence through school and life chances. A recent report published by the Annie Casey Foundation[6] finds that children who do not read proficiently by the end of third grade are four times more likely to leave high school without a diploma. Securing a job with livable wages without a high school diploma is a challenge, to put it mildly. As a result, young people sometimes find it necessary to engage in unlawful underground economies in order to survive, and then we imprison them.

Thus, the withholding of education is a political tool used to maintain and ensure an economic and social underclass. This underclass is defined overwhelmingly by race, disproportionately comprised of black and brown people because of the disproportionate degree to which young people of color are criminalized and pushed out of school. In this way, schools are deeply implicated in the systematic maintenance of the racialized American caste system.[7]

This is a continuation of America's historic legacy of injustice. In the era of slavery, teaching a black person to read was illegal because reading and writing are forms of power, tools for organizing, means to freedom. Removing young children from school, hindering their capacity to acquire such tools, inevitably relegates certain young people—black and brown people, in particular—to a life in modern-day chains.

In short, the policies and practices that we use to discipline children—starting in the earliest grades—have the potential to set off the first in a long line of falling dominoes that might end in a young person facing the direst of circumstances. The consequences of these unjust practices, however, are neither solely individual nor solely economic. If schools fail to offer young people the chance to imagine freedom, to practice freedom, and to prepare for freedom, it is unlikely that these young people will prove able to create the free country human beings deserve. It may be difficult for a kindergarten teacher to understand the potential impact of her everyday treatment of Anthony on his future life chances and on our collective struggle for freedom, but drawing that connection has begun to take hold in educational research, and it must begin to take stronger hold in everyday teaching practice.

Since beginning my career as a public school teacher and meeting Anthony, I have learned a lot about power and authority, about young children, about what it means to teach and learn, and about what it means to be human in a school building. While completing my doctorate in education I served as director of elementary education at Brown University and at Wellesley College, preparing cohorts of new teachers—and learning so much with and from them. I have since moved to Michigan to continue my research on what teaching has to do with freedom. Perhaps most important, I became a co-parent to my life partner's two wonderful young boys. In this role, above any of my professional roles, I have felt the firsthand urgency of the need for schools more deserving of our children.

Over these many years, I have worked with novice elementary school teachers and their mentors in and around Providence, Boston, and Detroit. I supported their work in public, private, and charter school classrooms; in suburban, urban, and rural classrooms; in multiracial and deeply segregated schools; in progressive and very traditional schools. Despite wide variation in many characteristics of these schools and classrooms, I can always walk into the teachers' lounge and hear the educators complaining to one another about their Anthony. I find Anthony sitting alone in all of these hallways, looking forlorn. I see him at a time-out desk in the back of the classroom, facing the wall. I catch glimpses of him waiting with the secretary for his lecture from the principal.

Indeed, it rarely takes me more than five minutes in a classroom to figure out which child is Anthony. Sometimes teachers apologize on Anthony's behalf before I even spot him for myself. My student teachers want nothing more than to know what to do about Anthony.

This book is interested in Anthony, certainly, and in kids like him, but not in what to do about him. I am concerned instead with what we might learn *from* him about what to do with, and for, all of our children.

In this spirit, the following chapters are portraits of Zora, Lucas, Sean, and Marcus—first and second graders who regularly failed to comply with the demands of their teachers. I found these children by first asking principals to identify their strongest teachers, and then asking those teachers to identify the children posing the most challenging behaviors. It does not matter whether or not these children were "objectively" challenging by some external standard; indeed, placed in different classrooms or schools, they might not be similarly flagged. A "problem child" in one place may go unnoticed in another. What matters is their teachers' identification, and the resulting interaction between the children and that identification.

I used portraiture,[8] a research methodology developed by Sara Lawrence-Lightfoot, to document the experiences of these children. This approach begins by asking, *What is good here?* This search for goodness was particularly helpful in providing the empathic approach necessary to lovingly understand children so often understood as "bad." It prompted me to recognize the need to see these four children outside of school, to wonder who they were in other settings. So in addition to seeing the children in their classrooms, I also shadowed them in the other parts of their lives—at home with their grandmas and pets, at the park with their siblings and friends, in karate class. No doubt you will recognize something familiar in these portraits. In them, you will see yourself, your own children, the children you know, or the children you've taught.

Importantly, I intentionally include children who differ based on race, gender, and class. All children respond to the arrangements of school, and these responses are strongly mediated by the children's identities (and the teachers' identities). We can learn something about when, whether, and how identities matter in children's interactions with school by including some diversity. Still, it is crucial to continue to acknowledge that young people of color are disproportionately impacted by disciplinary malpractice in schools, and that the ongoing supremacy of whiteness is arguably the most toxic of poisons in the air of our school buildings.

Zora and Lucas attend a relatively wealthy, predominantly white school in the suburbs, while Sean and Marcus attend school in a city that is uniquely racially and socioeconomically diverse. Troublemaking is not unique to "urban" classrooms, despite the disproportionately vigilant spotlight on city schools in the media and in scholarly research. My view is that all children interact with the particular arrangements of their schools, and there is something to learn from how different types of schools arrange their cultures differently. In any kind of school, some children will be practicing the act of refusal.

As you read the portraits of Zora, Lucas, Sean, and Marcus—as you begin to learn a bit about what they are like both at school and at home—I hope you will try hard to hear them, to mine their experiences for lessons on freedom. I ask that you try to view them as canaries tasked with protecting the miners, young people who are being sacrificed, ostensibly for our collective benefit.

These children make otherwise invisible harm both visible and audible, and even if noncompliance is a threat to their own wellbeing, they persist in signaling the danger. We generally think of "deviance," and of deviant people, as a problem. I have learned to think of deviance as informative, and often as an exercise of power and free will. The child who deviates, who refuses to be-have like everybody else, may be telling us—loudly, visibly, and memorably—that the arrangements of our schools are harmful to human beings. Something toxic is in the air, and these children refuse to inhale it. It is dangerous to exclude these children, to silence their warnings.

The idea of the miners' canary fundamentally changed my under-standing of misbehavior. I began to think more critically about the requirement of obedience in schools. Should one *not* make trouble if one's dignity requires it? Should we *not* teach children that some-times there is a need to break rules, a need to challenge authority, a need to refuse inhumane conditions and arrangements, a need for organized, collective disobedience?

Many are hesitant to assign agency to very young children, and we could engage a debate about the level of consciousness they leverage in their everyday noncompliance. But behaviors are social actions—they happen within social interactions—and children's behavior is a response to context regardless of whether that re-sponse is voluntary or involuntary, intentional or unintentional. Every time a child breaks a rule, never mind the purposefulness or lack thereof, she exercises her human right *not* to comply, and she signals something about the demand she refuses to meet. Maybe she can't meet the demand. Maybe she can but doesn't want to. Whatever the case, her noncompliance marks the need to evaluate the demand, not just the child. And her behavior reminds us of her power.

Zora, Lucas, Sean, and Marcus each teach us something im-portant, powerful, and worthy about how to reimagine classrooms in the image of being fully human, and how to teach love and learn freedom. They offer lessons on power and authority, loneliness and belonging, creativity and conformity. Their experiences and in-sights draw our attention away from the confinement of pathology and toward the complexity of goodness; away from blame and toward understanding; away from evaluation and toward curiosity. They teach us about how schools—not just children—make trouble. And they sing freedom, with the hope of being released from their cages.

Part One

Forest School

FOR NEARLY FIFTEEN YEARS, Jane Norbert and Nancy Beverly have worked as partner teachers in adjacent classrooms at Forest Elementary School. Winding suburban roads, framed on both sides by large houses and thick patches of trees, lead to the school. Upon entering the school building, visitors are welcomed by the bright and colorful works of young artists—self-portraits done in collage, insects created with computer software, kites designed to test children's understanding of symmetry. Security consists of checking in at the main office and wearing a neon sticky badge, and there is often a crowd gathered around the sign-in sheet since scores of parents seem frequently to have reasons to stick around during the day.

Fierce advocates of multi-age classrooms, Mrs. Norbert and Mrs. Beverly teach a mix of first and second graders, who are with them for two years. They are educational veterans, each having taught for almost two decades now, and they are not only professional collaborators but also extraordinarily close friends. Though a door connects one classroom to the other, it almost always remains open. Both teachers and their students move fluidly between the two-in-one learning space, and visitors always know to check both rooms in search of any particular child.

The only time the connecting door will close is in the rare instance when a whole-class lesson is taking place, one in which
quiet and focused concentration are required in separate areas.
Then Mrs. Norbert has no choice but to shut that door so she can
be heard over Mrs. Beverly's voice on the other side of the wall.
Mrs. Beverly is loud. Her voice is strong and powerful, as is her
physique. She stands tall and straight, a white woman with long,
thick blond hair and a distinctive sense of style. Bright colors in
bold combinations are accented by interesting and eye-catching
accessories—a leather belt with a deep turquoise stone in its center; dangling earrings made by Indian artisans with recycled materials; distinctive shoes with a high wedge or multiple straps; a
necklace featuring a beetle preserved in a glass oval.

Mrs. Beverly's athletic build is the result of her deep love of the
outdoors and all things physical. She is a lifelong swimmer and a
hiker, a nature aficionado and outdoor expert who can easily identify any plant, seed, or animal print left in dirt or snow. After two
years in her class, the seven-year-olds who leave for third grade
inevitably share her knowledge and passion. "Asiatic bittersweet,"
a second grader tells me on one of the many nature walks we take
as a class in the surrounding woods. Pointing with disapproval to
these climbing vines of bittersweet, he tells me, "Those will strangle that tree. They need to be cut."

Mrs. Beverly's physical presence—confident, striking, powerful—
matches her tone in the classroom. Her many years of experience
bolster her identity as a master teacher, and her leadership within
the school and at the district level is well established. She and
Mrs. Norbert are the grade-level liaisons on many committees, and
they often co-lead professional development sessions for other teachers. Mrs. Beverly has a clear vision and set of values embedded in her
approach to curriculum, pedagogy, and classroom management—
and she does not waver in her defense of them. Mrs. Beverly is not

to be trifled with. Everyone understands this, including kids, their parents, other teachers, and the administrators.

Mrs. Norbert, by contrast, though equally firm in her values and beliefs, has a softer style. A mother of two children who are students at the school, she has a more empathetic relationship to the community of parents, and a slightly higher threshold of patience for children who step out of line. But in no way is she soft. Like Mrs. Beverly, she has a strong presence as the leader and authority of her classroom space. She is also white, with a short bob of light brown hair and a more casual choice of dress—usually khakis or chino pants with a floral or solid long-sleeved T. Mrs. Norbert is a talented artist and a perfectionist. The charts she creates during a lesson are carefully and meticulously drafted. She keeps white-out tape at the side of her easel to immediately address errors, and she writes carefully and neatly, always thinking about the end product as she works to construct something worthy of her walls. Her hanging alphabet is hand-drawn, her calendar a beautifully constructed wood creation.

Unsurprisingly, Mrs. Norbert and Mrs. Beverly do not run traditional classrooms in which children are seated at desks, working independently. Despite an educational climate that increasingly scripts curricula through prepackaged materials and demands the standardization of teaching and learning, this veteran pair has managed to continue to color outside of those lines. Their status as master teachers, as well as the relative freedom they enjoy in the context of an affluent, well-performing suburban school, affords them the opportunity to more or less do as they please.

So, in keeping with their graduate-level training—which included a great deal of emphasis on children with special needs—as well as their personal philosophies about how children best learn, the curriculum and pedagogy they use are multisensory and multimodal. Through "studies"—lengthy units around a theme that integrate content areas—these teachers organize a rich curriculum for children. Within the course of a study, children are required to read and to write, to sing and to dance, to draw and to paint, to build and to create, to count and to measure, to jump and run and speak, and to listen and perform and reflect.

These are generally bustling, messy, deeply active classrooms in which children largely work together. Students travel from station to station across the two rooms for hours of the school day—grinding corn by hand during a study of indigenous peoples, writing myths during Greek study, comparing and contrasting Western and Eastern notions during Dragon study, stitching saris during a study inspired by Mrs. Beverly's recent travel to India. There are watercolors and music, cooking materials and objects for sewing, and books upon books.

Mrs. Beverly's classroom, in particular, looks lived-in; there are piles of stuff everywhere, whole tables covered with materials and disorganized bins, scraps of paper all over the floor. Mrs. Norbert's is more carefully monitored for neatness. But both teachers have one clear and unobstructed spot in their rooms: director's chairs at the front with their names stitched into the canvas.

There is no mistaking who is in charge.

Despite the general hustle and bustle, there are also many times when the young learners are required to sit still, silently and patiently, for a read-aloud or a share-around, sometimes with all fifty children in one crammed space. They often sit for more than an hour straight, pretzel-style on the rug, with very clear, even rigid, expectations for their behavior. *Sit up straight. Don't fuss with things in your hands. Fold your legs in. Don't dare interrupt.* The children are being trained as both audience and presenters, and they are actively coached in these roles. When six-year-old Carmen stretches her arms in an awkward way while timidly presenting her work, she is repeatedly coached—in front of all forty-nine of the other children and by both teachers in tag-team fashion—to "stop it with the arms," to "speak up," to "stop making that face." When another child walks back to his spot with a serious hunch in his shoulders and arms dragging at his sides, he is made to return to the center of the circle, walk again, and yet again, until he is upright to his teachers' satisfaction.

High expectations for behavior are coupled with high levels of academic rigor. These are teachers who talk to and treat young learners as fully capable beings. Their read-alouds are often chapter books of more than three hundred pages intended for an older audience in which vocabulary is advanced, story lines are complex, and the required inferences are subtle. The small children are deeply engrossed in these lengthy stories, eagerly awaiting read-aloud time and often begging to continue when time is up. Ongoing, often informal comprehension instruction supports their capacity to understand the works. "See, here's where you really have to do the heavy lifting of reading," says Mrs. Beverly during one read-aloud session. "You have to put together everything you know about this character's personality to understand this action, this individual's temerity."

A rich, rigorous, and engaging curriculum that values creativity and multiple ways of knowing is juxtaposed with a consistent and sometimes harsh reminder that there are rigid rules, norms, codes of behavior, that mustn't be challenged if one wants to be successful in this setting. Both teachers regularly use public scolding and high-volume redirection, and Mrs. Beverly is particularly unapologetic about her choice of a harsh management style. To explain it, she says, "I have to sort of bring them into a place where their behavior is commensurate with expectations of the classroom because this is a white-bread Americana school."

Forest is, indeed, a white-bread American school. There is a handful of children of color in each classroom, generally no more than three in a class of twenty-five. There is not a single teacher of color, nor any staff members, save one member of the janitorial team. The surrounding community is home to a small liberal arts college, where 66 percent of the adult population holds an advanced degree beyond a bachelor's and just 2 percent of families live below the poverty line. Generally, the children come from well-resourced families in which it is common for only one parent to work.

There are clear ways of being in this school space, cultural norms and codes that signal upper-class academia and white professionalism, for children and teachers alike. Those who cannot or will not adhere to these standards will inevitably be flagged as problematic. This is the case for both Zora and Lucas, the two children whose portraits follow.

Zora

On Being Out-Standing

Take the First Step

"This way to my room," says Zora Williams, authoritatively leading me to the second floor of her house. "Try to hurry." A wide, tall staircase leads from one level to the next, and Zora's mom has painted a phrase on each step—a collection of fourteen altogether, an explicit code of conduct that the family sees each day. *Love yourself. Express yourself. Be fearless. Do your best. Keep your promises. Stand tall. Don't be afraid to apologize. Say I love you.*

Appropriately, the first stair reads, *Take the first step.* I am visiting Zora at home in the first week of summer, after many long months of seeing her at school. My first day with Zora—our first step together in this project—was her first day of second grade. We were both late. I was hustling through the hallway trying not to spill my coffee and she was running just ahead of me in her shiny new Nikes—black slip-ons with a neon pink swoosh. She moved quickly, tall for her age, and lean. But her movement was more wild than graceful: elbows out, each pace dramatic and exaggerated, like a cartoon character being chased through thick brush.

She was dressed for a special occasion that day. Her hair was in a collection of tight twists with multicolored rubber bands, and someone had taken great care to create a perfect zigzag part down the center. She'd donned a zip-up green hoodie with a matching pink tennis dress. Bright brown eyes were shining behind funky purple eyeglasses.

It was impossible not to find her adorable.

Zora throws her backpack hastily on a hook and darts inside the classroom. She is familiar with the room since she spent the year prior with Mrs. Beverly as well, but half the crop of children will be new as incoming first graders. She scans the group, as I do, and I wonder what she's noticing or looking for. I can't help but see that hers is the only brown face in a sea of white. She has a gorgeous caramel complexion—a blend of her Puerto Rican mother and African American father. Here, she stands out, but her skin color isn't the only reason. The other children are already seated together on the rug listening to the teacher, and they all turn to stare at the latecomer. Mrs. Beverly stands up from her director's chair and beelines over to Zora, giving a quick welcome and instructions. In her first five minutes at school, attention has already been drawn to Zora Williams.

Considering how much attention she was paid during kindergarten and first grade, so much of it negative, I wonder if there will be very much new about this year.

Zora is asked to add her vote to the class survey, part of the morning ritual in which a question is posed for children to consider: *How did you feel when you woke up this morning?* The options for a response are *excited, nervous, both,* or *other.* Eleven children are excited. One is nervous. "What could *other* be?" asks Zora, interrupting the class discussion already in progress. "You mean angry? Or maybe lazy?" I fear the interruption will result in a negative consequence, but to my surprise Mrs. Beverly responds by engaging the other children for their ideas.

"You could be just plain scared," offers one first grader.

"I was crying," says another.

The first day of school, like a holiday, is often filled with much ritual and emotion. In some households, outfits are carefully chosen the night before, and shiny new lunch boxes and sneakers sit at front doors, sometimes for several days to build anticipation. Photos are taken, capturing that quintessential image of a tiny person with a giant backpack, a big smile with holes where baby teeth have fallen out.

But in many other households, the first day of school is a day of dread and nerves. For the families of children who struggle, battling daily with behavior problems or academic frustration, early September is a difficult time. As Zora places her vote on *excited*, I wonder how she and her family have really been feeling in the days leading up to this first step.

I met Zora, briefly, during the previous school year when I was supervising a student-teaching intern in Mrs. Beverly's classroom. The first time I visited I opened the classroom door right into the back of a small child—Zora Williams sitting outside of the group during a time-out for noncompliance. I knew the intern and teacher were concerned about this child, but seeing this one brown face (further) excluded from her peers made my stomach tight. She looked alone, and so very different.

A full year later, there had been much growth. Zora had grown. Mrs. Beverly's knowledge of Zora had grown. The relationship between the two of them had grown. I had hoped this might mean a new beginning for everyone. Yet, on just this first day of school, the number of times Zora's name was spoken by Mrs. Beverly suggested another challenging year lay ahead.

"Zora, can you stand up please so I can see your face?"

"Zora, are those Legos cleaned up?"

"Zora, you're starting to talk again."

"Zora, this is the third time I've had to ask you to come here."

"Zora, I'd hate to take your recess on the first day of school."

"Zora, you're the only person whose body is not facing the direction I want it in."

"Zora, I'm waiting for eye contact right now."

"Zora, we're all over here. What are you doing?"

By the end of the day, I am tired. Mrs. Beverly is tired. Zora is tired. We're on the first step, intimidated by the long climb ahead.

One hundred and seventy-nine days to go.

Love Yourself

"How do we want our classroom to be?" asks Mrs. Beverly. She is at her easel with marker in hand, the children gathered on the rug to begin the work of developing a set of shared rules for the year. "How do we want people to treat each other? How do we want the classroom environment to be when it's a work time? How do you want to feel when you walk in every morning? Those are the kinds of rules I want. This is *your* space, and for some of you it will be your space for two more years."

The children offer their thoughts. They're young but already well versed in the norms of classroom life and the words they know their teachers want to hear. The rules flow freely as the kids parrot what so many classroom rules sound like. *Keep the classroom green and clean. Respect other people. Respect the materials. Share. Treat people the way you want to be treated.* "Don't keep somebody lonely," offers one little girl. "Like, in a corner."

"How do we want to write that?" asks Mrs. Beverly, looking for raised hands.

Zora calls out. "Comfort somebody."

Mrs. Beverly ignores the contribution, with a look in Zora's direction that signals she should have raised her hand. She calls on another child, who says that if someone is lonely, you should ask the person to play with you. Zora, who had been disengaged from the conversation until this idea of loneliness was raised, again calls out. She's eager on this point. "Comfort someone if they're alone. Maybe not if they're very upset. We should let them calm down a little first. But then comfort them."

It doesn't surprise me that this rule feels important to her. Zora lives a lonely life on the margins of her school community. She is different, caught in the intersections of identity. She's biracial, bicultural, and working toward becoming bilingual. And though her parents have money, they didn't come from money. She doesn't fit the rigid demographics of her class, which is overwhelmingly white, English only, and intergenerationally affluent.

While the other girls sit together, play together, and choose to work together, Zora is not included. She is bold, physical, active, exploding with a seemingly uncontainable level of energy. She needs to move and is excited by rough-and-tumble play. She loves video games and action figures, loud sound effects and fierce pretend battles. This makes her better suited for the kind of play the young boys in her class engage in, and she often seeks them out despite the fact that her classmates tend to segregate themselves into single-sex playgroups. Zora challenges this norm.

Yet, she doesn't quite fit with the boys, either. Though her style of play suits them, her personality does not. Zora is authoritative and disregards the established social hierarchy that exists within the boys' group. She overrules the alpha males with her own wants and ideas, her own rules for how games should be played. She doesn't care that she lacks the unspoken social permission to be in charge of them, and she often tries to take control. This results in her exclusion from the boys' play as well.

For an observer, it hurts to witness her struggle for a place at the social center. At recess, I watch Zora try to enter an all-boys game of tag. The boy who is "it," a well-respected and popular child, vigorously chases another revered male peer. Though a variety of boys are playing and many are much closer and easier to tag, this unnecessarily challenging pursuit continues.

Zora, rather than running away from the boy who is "it," runs toward him. *She* is chasing *him*. "Tag me!" she yells repeatedly. "Here I am! Get me!" Over and over she relentlessly repeats her command, which he systematically ignores despite the fact that she is easily within reach. It is painful to watch.

After a few futile minutes, she leaves the organized game and seeks out a comrade on the margins: a heavyset boy who is generally stuck playing with one of the paraprofessionals. He is an easy-going personality and loves to chase her even though she is super speedy and there is no chance of catching her. She dominates the play and he accepts her commands easily. As a result, they appear to enjoy a wonderful playtime together.

Yet, every day I watch her first try to enter the mainstream games without success. She doesn't seem to accept life on the margins, where she might create her own parallel play space with a hodge-podge of comrades. Rather, I watch her struggle futilely for a place at the dominant center. At lunch, in the cafeteria, she wanders around every day before landing inevitably at the last table, for all the kids who don't have a seat in the other circles. Hers is the only table mixed by race and gender. At choice time, while the other children immediately seek out the peers they play with each day, she doesn't have a place and often ends up alone after some kind of altercation resulting from an attempt to insert herself, uninvited, into another group's activity. When the children are allowed to choose their own work partners I see her body stiffen up, as she is likely anticipating the difficulty she will have finding someone with whom she can work.

Much of Zora's work time gets spent in attempts to entertain and amuse the other children. "Have you guys ever seen a moth close up? Like, *really* close up?" She is diligently working to distract the others while they do scientific drawings of butterflies. "The first time I saw a moth's eyeballs close up, I screamed my pants off."

She looks around for the reaction.

Nothing.

So she repeats herself, but this time with dramatic flair: "I was like, ahhhhhhhh!" She pretends her pants are falling off while she struggles embarrassedly to keep them on. This gets the table going, and she appears to be feeling encouraged. "Hey, look, my drawing looks like this butterfly is singing and dancing on the flower!" She does a purposely silly, exaggerated jig. The kids crack up and she looks quite pleased with herself. Of course, now all the noise draws attention to the table and the teacher reprimands her. She is behind in her work and creating a deliberate distraction for the others. But she seems completely unaffected by getting in trouble, as though the opportunity to interact in a positive way with the other children was well worth the gamble of a negative consequence.

This strategy, of playing the role of entertainer in the classroom, is one Zora relies on quite a bit despite the fact that it so often results in trouble. She doesn't seem to have very many alternate strategies. Because she spends a lot of time alone, and because she is so often in trouble and then further excluded from the group for creating distractions, she doesn't get the opportunity to practice the social skills necessary for building and maintaining close relationships. "She nudges people relentlessly," says Mrs. Beverly. Being the group entertainer works well because she gets to be the center of attention *and* she gets to direct the scene onstage. But in close friendships, where there is a requirement for reciprocity, compromise, and give-and-take, she struggles to yield to other people's desires.

Zora has a thorny and complicated friendship with another child on the outskirts of social life in Room 1/2A—a boy named Tyler. These two are so often alone that coming together seems sensible, but their strong personalities in combination with their lack

of practice in social skills creates a volatile dynamic. I arrive at recess one day to find Zora screaming in Tyler's face. "I will *never*—I
repeat, never, ever, ever—play with you again! You are the worst.
Do you hear me? Never! Don't. Ever. Come. Near. Me. Again!" I
had never seen her so angry before, and never saw her so angry
again. It was a deep-down anger, the kind that comes from a deep-
down pain. She stormed away, still muttering to herself, and was
unreachable.

When I asked Tyler what had happened, he shrugged his shoulders. "I have no idea. Who knows with her?"

Mrs. Beverly describes their relationship as one with a "push-
pull" dynamic, one in which they need each other and are drawn
together, but also one full of "nudging" and competition for authority. Tyler is the only child whom I ever heard Zora call a friend. At
the end of both first and second grade, the children are asked to
write reflective letters to themselves to include in their portfolios,
summarizing the key moments and memories of the year that has
passed. Zora includes Tyler in her short letters to self, in both first
and second grade:

Dear Zora,
When you were in first grade you loved Greek study. Because
you were very musicale. And you loved your teacher alot. Because your teacher taught you alot of lesons. And you love
playing with your pal Tyler at reecs.
Love, Zora

At first she wrote that she "loved" playing with Tyler at recess, but
then she scribbled out the "d" to make it present tense.

Dear Zora,
When you were in second grade you played with your Best pal
Tyler. You played with him a lot. Evrey day you met up at the

play strucsher and played. You also had a favorite speshalest called gym. You liked it because it could get you fit and healthy. You also had a big event. You met with your pen pals, you played on the strucsher with them, you even saw a spider on the strucsher and you even said Hi to it. And you thougt it was haveing fun. Oh, there were lots of things you did, but its getting to the end of the year. So your self just wanted to remind you of all of the things you did before the end of the year.

Sicerly, Zora Williams, from 1-2A

As Zora reflects on the most important aspects of her year, this special friend—whom I saw her fight with more often than not—receives attention and mention. The friendship is obviously important to her. She seems to sense their alignment intuitively, their shared position on the margins. At the same time, the relationship is a problematic one that leaves both without positive peer modeling of the skills required for friendship.

When asked to photograph a few of her favorite things, Zora captures an image of a toy that she explains is very important to her—a plush little remote control dog that can move and behave in other quite human ways. "I love him," she explains. "Because he is always ready to play and he does what I want." Even when I am with her at home and ready to play, she chooses the dog's company over mine.

Living on the margins while refusing to embrace social norms leaves Zora without peer friendships or a genuine space of belonging. It must be lonely. While the other children are integrated into the fabric of classroom social life, hers is a loose and isolated thread. I often wonder if her disruptive behavior signals a desire to be seen, recognized, made central. Though her skin color makes her highly visible, classroom social life carries on as if she's not there. It seems that the more she feels left out and invisible, the more she engages in behavior that actively draws the attention of others.

She is most often in trouble for the kinds of things that signal a desire to be noticed: calling out, being silly at the wrong times, failing to complete work because she has created entertaining distractions. "Even when she's calling something out," explains Mrs. Beverly, "it's not something that's a non sequitur. It's usually something that's kind of a smart-alecky remark but would make people laugh. And so she has kids enjoying her at the same time where I might be, like, you need to raise your hand."

As entertaining as she can be, the trouble she gets in signals to her peers that she is a problem. "She has a reputation as public enemy number one," Mrs. Beverly tells me. The reputation harms her relationships with both adults and children and stems from her earliest days at the school. During her kindergarten year, Zora struggled so severely that her parents tell me they considered removing her from school altogether. She regularly refused to comply with the mandates of the classroom—calling out and speaking out of turn, failing to complete assigned work, getting out of her seat to wander toward others, engaging in altercations and arguments with her classmates, actively and passively refusing to follow directions.

Her exasperated kindergarten teacher requested a paraprofessional to shadow Zora throughout the day. In this way, her behavior won her at least the full-time attention of one adult. She spent a significant amount of instructional time wandering the hallways with the paraprofessional on time-outs. The individualized attention and time away from class may have been emotionally preferable to the demands of classroom life. But she missed key and formative academic content, and the other children—looking on— internalized a harsh judgment of her.

When Zora entered first grade with Mrs. Beverly, the memory of kindergarten lay heavy in the air—and Mrs. Beverly was determined to improve Zora's behavior while refusing to physically exclude her. "I spent all summer thinking about how I was going to keep this kid in the room," she says. But keeping her in the classroom did not mean she was included. Because her transgressions and the resulting redirection were often loud and public, daily and ongoing, her reputation as public enemy—in the eyes of her peers, especially—went unchallenged. This made social life more difficult and threatened Zora's ability to love herself. Though she was no longer physically removed from the classroom, she remained on the social outskirts.

As if to forge her own identity as a likable member of the classroom community, on her own terms, Zora regularly leveraged disruption as a way to entertain her peers. When children laughed at her jokes and her theater, she felt liked by them and, in turn, liked herself. For Zora, these feelings appeared to be worth the trouble.

Express Yourself

The children are working on decorating one of their subject folders for the year. Mrs. Beverly has provided piles upon piles of animal photos cut from magazines. The children are to select from these and create collages on their folders, and as I scan the room the majority of children have dutifully followed the directions. Many are finished with the task before Zora has begun.

Zora picks up a picture of a seagull. She utters a series of very realistic-sounding seagull squawks while launching the photo into the air as though the bird has taken flight. It lands on her classmate's head. "Oops," she says, with a sly grin and a cartoonish bird voice. "It made an unpleasant deposit on your shoulder."

I hold back my laughter, and the child's displeased reaction draws Mrs. Beverly's attention. "Get to work, Zora. Or you'll be finishing during recess." The threat is motivating, and Zora sets about the task with more seriousness. Still, her work time includes many interludes during which animals battle one another, move together, talk trash, even give birth. The straightforward and constrained task is injected with her imagination, creativity, and dramatic flair.

Most of the children select a favorite animal and glue it in the center. Some overachievers make sensible additions of other animal friends that might be found with this central favorite. Zora, scanning both sides of each provided cutout, manages to locate a non-animal option: a large bust of some historical male royalty in costume. She immediately glues him to the folder. With purpose and clear intention now, she flips through the piles, locating any and all small birds. This requires that she move from table to table rather than stay seated, and she is again reprimanded. But the redirection does not deter her from her mission; she persists in collecting small birds anywhere she can find them, to the dismay of her classmates, who are often fishing through the pile when she grabs a picture from their stack. Sometimes she grabs an image right out of their hands.

In the end, her folder features an eccentric collection of small birds perched on the shoulders of royalty. Her work stands out. It is *out-standing*.

On another occasion the children are asked to border their name tags with a pattern. She begins immediately and, again, with purpose. Thunderbolt, heart, thunderbolt, heart, thunderbolt, heart. "Why thunderbolts?" I ask, considering it an unusual choice.

"For Zeus," replies Zora. "That's his symbol. And the hearts are for Aphrodite, the goddess of love." Her pattern stands out as she applies what she learned in Greek study the year before. She simply cannot help but bring brilliance and flair, even to mundane assignments.

A visit to Zora's home makes clear some of the roots of that flair. Her house sits at the end of a long driveway, so far back that it isn't immediately visible from the street. But once you see it, you can't miss it. It stands out.

A fenced gate at the side of the house is painted in multiple colors, each post different from the next. A careful design is painted around the gate itself, an elaborate icon designed out of the first initial of each family member's name. I am greeted at the door by Zora's Puerto Rican grandmother from New York City—a lively, loud, exuberant force in a patterned sundress, tight curls, and wide smile. She is chatting me up excitedly, proudly introducing the features of the home. The television is on. A teenage uncle and brother are in the house someplace. A large dog in some kind of neck brace is getting at me. The other grandmother is coming to town. The mom is urging Zora to avoid distraction and finish her lunch. Shoes crowd the entryway and a sign at the door instructs visitors to use the hand sanitizer provided.

There is a lot to take in.

No inch of wall has been spared from the life of this family: words painted, photographs framed, artwork hanging. A giant, beautifully painted portrait of the mother and father on their wedding day—barefoot at the beach with the husband's arms around the wife's waist—is prominently featured. The mother, an artist, has been busy in this house. The stairs are painted. The doorknobs are painted. The dining table is hand carved and painted.

To enter Zora's room is to feel as if you are entering the scene of a beautifully chaotic fairy tale. An angled ceiling is painted yellow, accented busily with decals of planets and stars. The other walls are a bright coral, also featuring stickers and pictures and other décor. Glittery purple lace is draped from one side of the room to the other. A canopy bed with a printed quilt sits atop a bright, patterned area rug. One entire side of the room is filled with gigantic bins of toys and stuffed animals, and a comfy pink reading chair sits in the corner under a tall lamp, shaded by three oversized silk flowers. Objects around the room are labeled in both English and Spanish.

The door to Zora's room is painted coral, with a turquoise and yellow square in the center. A wreath hangs with pink and purple flowers. Below that, a poster is featured with a quote paraphrased from Karl Marx: *Philosophers have sought to understand the world. The point, however, was to change it.*

Pictures of and quotes by prominent African American heroines and heroes hang above Zora's desk—a reminder of those who came before as she sets about her own work. A thank-you note from Mrs. Beverly is pinned to a corkboard, acknowledging a holiday gift from the family: *The bright and lovely colors remind me of you.*

And alongside the card are some words to Zora from her mother: *You are beautiful just the way you are.*

The home is wonderfully chaotic: busy, active, hectic, lived-in, alive. It is the very opposite of mundane. These are not people trying to fit in.

But in her school life, Zora is encouraged to conform. "She already stands out as one of a small handful of African American faces here," Mrs. Beverly tells me. "I don't want her behavior to make her stand out even more." There is value in going unnoticed at school. Belonging is synonymous with blending in. "We work really hard across these two classrooms to make every child feel accepted, part of this community. And we work—Jane and I work really hard on behavior." To the teachers, working hard on behavior is working hard on making the children acceptable so they can be accepted. At home, though, Zora is encouraged to follow her own path, to be *out-standing*, to express herself, and to be proud of being different.

Zora's parents model standing out, and having pride in being different, as a strategic response to hostile and isolating environments. Zora's mom regularly attends school events, and I always notice how she stands out. The other moms are overwhelmingly white and are in careful and subdued outfits with simple hairstyles and laid-back looks. Mrs. Williams, in her turquoise capris and hot pink T-shirt, or her brightly patterned sundresses, or her body-fitting long red skirt, dons large earrings, painted nails, reddish curls in a high ponytail puff. She often sits or stands apart from the other parents.

I wonder if Zora's mom misses her old neighborhood in New York, where folks of color were the norm rather than the exception. When I ask if she ever feels lonely or isolated in her now predominantly white community, she smiles. "Nah," she says. "I notice how people around here sometimes look at me. It's like the way those girls in Zora's class look at her. With their noses up. But when I feel like they're judging me, looking at me like that, I just turn everything up a notch—I blast my music, turn up the heat on my accent, you know . . ." She laughs. "I'm like, here I am. Let me just put *all* this out there."

Her husband, too, can't be missed. He comes to a poetry reading by the children in a bright yellow corduroy blazer, lavender dress shirt, and a plaid, pastel-colored bow tie. Polka-dots on his socks. A spoken-word artist himself, he cheers all the children on loudly, proudly, calling out during their poems as is customary among artists in shared spaces—while the other parents clap politely and in measured time at each poem's end. In this context, and by his standards, calling out is not only appropriate, but required.

Rather than conform, these two leverage the act of being *out-standing* as a response to hostility, fully embracing a life and an identity at the margins. Coming of age in spaces where people of color were the majority, they enjoyed a sense of belonging in their formative years that ultimately bolstered the development of their strong, proud, and lively personalities. While her mom exaggerates her accent, and her dad dons his exceptionally bright clothing, they model an example of standing tall while standing out. It is as if to say, *We know you see us, so we'll give you something to look at.* It is a strategy they wish to pass along to Zora. *Stand tall. Express yourself. Love yourself.* For Zora, though, who is working hard to fit into an all-white space, being *out-standing* is punishable and ultimately isolating. Actively drawing attention to herself, refusing to conform or comply, is unwelcome behavior that strays from the norm.

Importantly, and to make matters more complicated, that norm reflects particular ways of being that will prepare the children at Zora's school for their assumed futures in white-dominated, affluent professions. There are particular ways to speak, to write, to interact with others. There are coveted skills and prized discourses, valued types of knowledge and celebrated modes of being. There is a culture to the classroom space. Mrs. Beverly and Mrs. Norbert often refer to this simply as "school culture," a neutral, normalized, and nonracialized term. But the presence of only a handful of children of color, who are more often in trouble than their white peers, prompts questions about the role of race. The very existence of these children forces the teachers to consider the possibility of racial factors, to be made aware of and self-conscious about their own whiteness.

Mrs. Beverly often worries aloud about whether her constant redirection is an attempt to make Zora "more white." She worries that the all-white space of the school encourages kids of color to get culturally "watered down": "Do I feel like 'White Teacher' sometimes? Yes. I feel it. I feel that I work in white suburbia. Our history with African Americans is such a dark one in so many ways. But I don't think Zora's parents would be happy for her to be at a charter, or some inner-city school that wasn't a high-flying one. So where do you find a school where there's more black culture, where it's black kids acting like black kids—not acting like the watered-down image of a white kid? And I do—those things do keep me up at night. And it's not just about Zora; it's about other kids of color that I've had. I think of all our kids of color here. Unfortunately, percentage-wise, more of them have behavior issues. And I don't know why that is."

Mrs. Beverly wrestles with the question of whether her strict enforcement of a particular way of being is racialized, going so far as to note the pattern at the school level in which kids of color are disproportionately in trouble. But she persists in that strict enforcement because she believes the demands of school life in grade three and beyond will require ever-increasing conformity to these behavioral expectations—the expectations of an overwhelmingly white, mainstream majority. Understanding that there are academic and economic rewards for meeting a standard of white, middle-class conformity, she cites those rewards as part of the motivation for enforcing a strict norm of behavior.

Her intentions are to hold Zora to the same standard as everyone else, regardless of color, even as she struggles with a discomfort that keeps her up nights. She feels that in doing so, she is readying Zora for a college experience and professional life that will likely demand the kinds of cultural behaviors and skills valued by the school. Her principled intentions, coupled with the troubling picture she paints of the "watered-down image of a white kid," remind me of Carter G. Woodson's words in the *Mis-Education of the Negro*:

> When a Negro has finished his education in our schools, then, he has been equipped to begin the life of an Americanized or Europeanized White man. . . . In this effort to imitate, however, these "educated people" are sincere. They hope to make the Negro conform quickly to the standard of the Whites and thus remove the pretext for the barriers between the races. They do not realize, however, that even if the Negroes do successfully imitate the Whites, nothing new has thereby been accomplished. You simply have a larger number of persons doing what others have been doing. The unusual gifts of the race have not thereby been developed, and an unwilling world, therefore, continues to wonder what the Negro is good for.[9]

I wonder how and where Zora's unusual gifts will get developed—
the cultural gifts passed down from her African and Puerto Rican
ancestors of color as well as those unique to her as an individual:
fierce creativity, a flair for the dramatic, uncontainable energy.

I also wonder how the other children, part of the "unwilling
world," will come to understand and appreciate Zora. Mrs. Beverly
expresses this worry as another motivation for coming down hard
on Zora's behavior. She worries that the other children—having
so few experiences with people of color—will form an association
in their minds between skin color and behavior: "Zora is African
American, and from absolutely proud parents who want her to be
totally intact as a person. And I just wonder what this would all
look like if Zora were in a different school where there was not so
much white-bread Americana. There have been times where I've
felt a little frustrated, I mean, it's not that I wouldn't call Zora out
on everything if her skin color were different. I'd be calling her on
it anyway. That's just who I am as a teacher. But there's times when
I am like, this is my one African American child who has heard
me say her name fifteen times—and what judgments are the kids
around her making? That's something that I've actually spoken to
her parents about. I've said, look, she's one of our few kids of color
in the entire school. You couple that with behavior that she's really
not quite able to manage, and that's where the heads are swiveling.
That's where kids are making assessments of their own."

Indeed, as I witness Zora's lonely life at school, I wonder how
these assessments prevent her from carving out a genuine space
of belonging. Her differentness is cause for isolation, even as her
parents encourage and celebrate their own differentness.

I wonder how a seven-year-old is to make sense of these simultaneous and conflicting messages. At home she is encouraged to be
out-standing and to embrace a life on the margins. Difference is
celebrated as a resource and a source of pride. At school she is encouraged to avoid drawing attention to herself, to find belonging in

the center of mainstream conformity. Difference is deviance, and deviance is punishable. Balancing the need to fit in with the reality of standing out is hard and taxing work. It is a burden Zora carries to school each day, a parallel and covert kind of teaching and learning she has to navigate. Her white peers do not share that burden and do not experience that same distraction to their academic learning. As Mrs. Beverly wonders aloud about the academic and social patterns that develop in the kids of color at Forest School, I think about this extra burden some children are forced to carry.

Be Fearless

"You know you're going to get in trouble if you get caught going that way, right?" We are on a nature walk through the forest surrounding the school, and Zora is taking a forbidden route around a fallen tree. The kids have been strictly warned, and she is falling behind the group significantly. I am feeling anxious, so I remind her that she is doing the wrong thing. She ignores me. I repeat myself. "Zora, you were told that you are not allowed to go that way." She ignores me again. The way of the fallen tree is so much more fun. It's slightly more treacherous and requires some jumping and problem solving. The path is not clear or easy, and in keeping with Zora's usual preference, adventure trumps the mundane. She trudges on. All the other children and adults are now completely out of sight, way ahead of us. When she clears the tree, I ask again, "You don't care about getting in trouble?"

"Don't worry so much," she replies. "You worry too much." And she takes off in a sprint to catch up with the rest of the group. Mrs. Beverly, who rarely misses a beat, sees her late arrival and begins to lay in. "We have all been gathered here for some time now, Zora. Do you want to explain why you have arrived so late? Did you imagine I wouldn't notice?" The scolding is loud, public, and severe. Zora sulks.

On the walk back to school Zora seems to pass the scolding forward, reprimanding other children for all kinds of transgressions. *You're too close to the street. Walk faster. Don't stop to pick things up; we're in a hurry. Tie your shoelace.* She mirrors the kind of authority modeled by the teacher, attempting to gain back some of the power she lost during her public reprimand. In the absence of reciprocal and equal relationships with her peers, she opts for one of assumed authority, and I often see that authoritative stance ramp up just after receiving a scolding. "She's one of the class bosses," another child tells me at lunch, with a tone of dislike.

"Is that true?" I ask Zora.

"Well, I prefer to think of myself as a junior assistant."

Zora is bold in pursuing her own desires—audacious at times—and doing so often requires that she wrestle with and negotiate not only the teacher's power over her, but also the power of her peers. "I'm waiting for a quiet table," Mrs. Beverly announces when the children are about to start decorating their writing folders. "The quietest table will be called up first to get their materials." Each group has a "head of table," and Zora's assigned leader is a white boy named Aidan. He takes his job very seriously. Zora is talking—telling a story to entertain her group—when she is supposed to be silent. Aidan puts the two-finger quiet signal directly in her face. I am struck by this white boy's audacity, and the raced and gendered undertones of the interaction. Infuriated, Zora loudly scolds him. They are both very frustrated with each other, and they glare at each other with angry eyes.

Zora then becomes fixated on the idea that a folder she has in her backpack could be her writing folder, instead of the one she is about to decorate. Her group still has not been called for supplies, thanks to the hullabaloo between her and Aidan. She begins to get up from the table to retrieve the folder from her backpack in the hallway, which is strictly forbidden for several reasons. She shouldn't be getting up at all since her entire group is still waiting to be called. Leaving the classroom right now will not be a good choice. "Zora!" Aidan looks like he is about to blow a gasket. She ignores him.

"What is it, Zora?!" Mrs. Beverly now shares Aidan's frustration.

"I have an *Angry Birds* folder in my backpack. That could be my writing folder."

"Do you think this is helping your group get called? I see Aidan, as your head of house, looking very frustrated! Get back to your seat."

When Zora returns to her spot, Aidan opens his mouth to say something. She puts her hand directly over his mouth: "Don't. Talk. To. Me. At. All," says Zora. She then puts her hands over her own face, as a way to disappear for a moment. Now, from the front of the classroom and across the entire space so as to be public, Mrs. Beverly continues her reprimand.

"Is your *Angry Birds* folder your writing folder, Zora?" It's a hypothetical question to which the answer should be "no."

"It *can* be," says Zora, challenging.

Mrs. Beverly is getting angrier. "But *is* it?"

"No."

"So did you really need to delay your whole group, and then get up to tell me about it?" Before Zora can answer she continues: "This is one of the things you're working on. Thinking to yourself, 'Do I need to do this?'" Zora's eyes get glassy. Aidan is at peace. It feels to me that Zora *did* need to get up to ask about that folder. Another child would not need to, perhaps, but her desire to retrieve that folder—to have it be her writing folder—felt urgent. Aidan's attempt to control her made that desire all the more pressing. And she tests Mrs. Beverly's power by trying to momentarily reason with her—"It *can* be." Ultimately, she is shut down by the teacher's power over her. And the entire event reinforces Aidan's power because he receives confirmation of his authority from the teacher, even though he failed to control Zora.

These incidents usually end badly for Zora, since neither Mrs. Beverly nor her peers miss any opportunity to reprimand and redirect her. Still, Zora fearlessly persists in pursuing her own desires, regardless of the predictable consequences. When she has a question, she blurts it out. Never mind the rule to raise hands or wait until questions are invited. When there is a butterfly outside the window, she gets up to look at it. Never mind that the teacher is in the middle of a whole-class lesson and Zora has chosen to leave the lesson without permission to catch a glimpse of it. When Zora wants to express a reaction to a read-aloud, she dramatically and loudly announces it. Never mind that she interrupts the reading and distracts the other twenty students with her expression.

Rules do not seem to impact Zora's decision-making process. Mrs. Beverly calls this "impulsive" and characterizes it as a lack of self-control. But it feels more to me like fearlessness. I think Zora considers the consequences and weighs the options, and then fearlessly decides to do what she wants anyway. As when she chose the dangerous and forbidden path on the nature walk, she refuses to "worry too much" about consequences.

At lunch one day, she is building what she excitedly calls a "super straw." Having grabbed more than ten straws from the cafeteria supply stack, she is connecting one to the next in a long string and she is planning on launching a spitball. The other children at the table are very interested, and this makes Zora all the more committed to her project. The paraprofessionals working the lunchroom, accustomed as they are to reprimanding her, are never too far away. "Zora, the rule is one straw. You know that because I've told you many times before." The paraprofessional begins to grab the pile of extra, unopened straws. Zora puts her hand on top of the adult's, to stop her.

"*Please!* I'm working on something! Please leave these alone! Walk away." Fearlessness.

"You know the rule," the adult patiently repeats, and she leaves with the tools for Zora's unfinished creation. I expect Zora to become upset, but instead she smiles slyly.

"Uh-huh!" she announces proudly, and pulls out a bunch of straws she was hiding under her leg on the chair. "She didn't see *these!*" And construction of the super straw commences. She doesn't seem at all fearful of getting caught. Indeed, I don't see her look up even once to check on the location of the adults. Her own project is paramount.

At just seven years old, Zora is already hypervisible and closely watched. The cafeteria paraprofessionals swarm around her, the recess ladies always have one eye keenly fixed on her, Mrs. Beverly always has her name in her mouth. She already stands out. She already has to negotiate the power exercised over her by others—adults and children alike.

Zora necessarily stands apart from her peers, and standing apart creates the possibility of standing below or above them. Though Mrs. Beverly is the clear authority, her reprimands serve as a model to the children for how to regulate the behavior of their peers. The children in Room 1/2A very often scold, redirect, and regulate one another, and they receive mixed messages about whether or not this is acceptable. On the one hand they are told only to "police yourself" and are sometimes reprimanded for bossing one another. On the other hand they are also told to "help each other do the right thing" and assigned positions of authority like "head of table," which become implicit and explicit encouragements to police one another.

When a peer wanders over to Zora's group during stations, Zora doesn't miss a beat: "Get back to work, Megan. You know where you're supposed to be." When she sees an aimless kindergartner in the hallway: "You shouldn't be out of class. Get back!" On another occasion, Zora scolds another child for sucking on her hair, and a commotion ensues during a lesson. The teacher says, "Police your-self," sternly, to Zora. But then she follows with a reprimand to the other girl. "But don't suck your hair. It will give you tangles." Zora has a look of satisfaction and redemption, which she passes to the other child in a gaze that silently says, *Told you so.*

Though Zora dishes out a good deal of peer scolding, she receives more of it than I can possibly capture. The children are often on her, mirroring the very language teachers use to redirect her. Zora is policed by her peers more than any other child in either of the two classes. During a single school day I recorded sixteen separate instances. In this way, she seems to stand below her peers. They feel they have the right, if not the duty, to exercise authority and power over her.

But Zora does not take these attempts at subjugation lightly. For every attempt to exercise power over her, there is an equal and reciprocal attempt to exercise her power over others. It is well es-tablished that she is fearless and authoritative. When pen pals from another school come to visit for the first time, it takes Zora's pen pal no more than ten minutes of interaction to conclude, "Sheesh, you are bossy!" It feels to me like a preemptive strike of some kind— the immediate desire to exercise power over, perhaps borne of the consistent disempowerment she experiences at the hands of both adults and her peers. She aligns herself with the role of a teacher, an authority, the "junior assistant."

This officious role, much like the entertainer role she often plays, can be seen as power and recognition. It is a way to be seen and to make herself visible that she controls and exercises at her own will; it is a counterattack, a response to the negative visibility that has been assigned to her and is beyond her control. These may not be positive ways to be seen, but at least they are identities she perceives to be choosing for herself.

Have Fun

Like all children, Zora wants an opportunity to enjoy the experience of school—to play, to be celebrated, to thrive, to belong. She wants to have fun. And she often feels that teachers stand in the way of that fun. When she takes to using jump ropes on the playground structure in a dangerous way, pretending they are horsewhips, she is reprimanded by the supervising teachers. "I'll never have my horses," she mutters to herself repeatedly. "Not with all these teachers around." To an adult, especially one tasked with keeping children within the bounds of reason and safety, her defiance can make her unlikable.

Mrs. Beverly is on point when she talks about the teacher she would like Zora to have in third grade, a teacher who is capable of seeing Zora's goodness: "Well, I think, here is a child who is loud, who is impulsive, who is a distraction to others. You've got to be able to like that kid. And if you can't like that kid from day one, she's not gonna feel that you like her or accept her in the room. And that sends a message to everyone else. As hard as I am on Zora, everyone knows that I like her. It's clear. It's even clear to her, and I think I'm harder on her than anyone. So, she needs someone who on day one is going to make her feel, *You are part of this classroom. I'm gonna stand by you. I am gonna scold you or I'm gonna guide you, but it's for your good. It's not because I don't like you.* And I think that, luckily, Zora is a likable kid. She is bright and funny and entertaining, but there are times where you want to strangle her because she is doing something that's absolutely not acceptable and taking six kids with her down that path."

Despite the obvious frustration that accompanies a difficult-to-manage child like Zora, Mrs. Beverly insists on the teacher's responsibility to stand by the child, to insist on her full participation, to like her. Still, though, and ironically, accepting the child means forcing the child into a particular definition of acceptable. To fully participate in the classroom community, to belong, Zora needs to be a point on the normal bell curve of behavior—not an outlier: "In a mixed-grade classroom, that behavior doesn't look so different because you get little kids in here who are still working on things. But in the third-grade classroom, it's gonna show more. In a straight-grade classroom, that spectrum of learning isn't as long as mine is. Straight-grade teachers are not as used to working on outliers, and Zora is an outlier in several places. She's made a lot of gains, but she's still an outlier, just in terms of habits of mind for school."

Some teachers work hard to manage children's behavior because they worry about how poor management will reflect on them as teachers. It is a self-interested motivation. For Mrs. Beverly, a veteran teacher with much experience and confidence, this is not at all the case. She has Zora's best interests at heart, even as she struggles with whether or not her constant redirection is problematic. "I see it as a quality-of-life issue," she says. "It must be exhausting to be so distracted and extreme, to have several movies always going on in your head at once."

Mrs. Beverly wants for Zora not to be an outlier. She wants her to be more normal, conforming, and compliant, so she can fit in and belong as a full, positive member of the classroom community. As a result, with the support of both Mrs. Norbert and the school psychologist, the issue of medication was raised to Zora's parents. Zora's impulsivity, her uncontainable energy, her insistence on adding flair to the mundane, is understood by the school as evidence of the possibility of attention deficit hyperactivity disorder (ADHD). I was present in a meeting where Zora's mother faced both of the teachers and the psychologist as they made their case for medication. The conversation focused on the "quality of life" Zora could enjoy if she were able to calm down a bit, fit in. They raised worry about her social skills. They raised worry about her math skills. They spoke of "impulsive" behaviors, with a multitude of examples, and they talked about children they had known for whom medication made a significant and positive difference.

Zora's mom couldn't deny the behaviors—the high energy, the feistiness, the creativity and dramatic flair that often distracted Zora from serious, hurried, or required tasks. "Yes, I have to remind her so many times to finish her breakfast or to get dressed. I know she's that way."

Against the backdrop of three school personnel presenting the evidence, making the case, it felt like persuasion more than discussion. Eventually, and with extreme hesitation, Zora's parents did start her on medication for ADHD. There were problems with the first attempt—weight loss and a dwindling appetite, a quiet and too-subdued Zora. Mrs. Beverly expressed her worry: "I don't want to lose the piece of Zora that is who she is, like her sense of humor, her kind of sassiness. I don't really want that to go away. And I have much sympathy and empathy for her parents. I know they want her off the meds. I know they totally want her off the meds. But off the meds, she does look super young and super out of control."

She was switched to an alternative medication.

When I asked Zora's parents about the medication over breakfast one morning, they talked about the struggle they faced in making the decision. Tears welled up in her mom's eyes. "I just—when it started to feel like she was falling behind, we got really worried."

As the medication calms her and she increasingly learns to fit the school norm as the years go by, I lament the potential loss of fun. What if things get dreary? Mundane tasks will retain their mundaneness. There will be no pretend animal battles, no silly jigs, no hilariously inappropriate jokes, no entertaining distractions and comic interludes. There will be no flair, dramatic or otherwise. She will trade adventurous and dangerous tree jumping in favor of a clear and easy path forward. Maybe she won't wear her father's bright colors. Maybe she won't splash her mother's artistic creativity on the walls of her own future home.

Maybe she will make good, predominantly white friends and finally find a desired place at the social center of her school. Maybe
she will thrive academically without distractions. Maybe she will
go on to fit easily into a college and professional life coded with
particular cultural standards for behavior. Maybe things will be
easier, less painful.

But will she have fun? Will she remain fearless? Will she be able
to love and express herself—in full and without hesitation? Will
she be free?

Back at the start of the school year the conversation about class
rules is wrapping up, the list coming to a close. Mrs. Beverly puts
the cap back on her marker. "Wait!" Zora exclaims, without raising
her hand, speaking out of turn. "We forgot another rule."

I'm surprised to see that Mrs. Beverly responds to her calling
out. "What is it?" she asks, opening her marker back up.

"Have fun."

That important rule is on one of the highest stairs in Zora's
home. Mrs. Beverly adds it.

"Put a heart and a star next to that one," says Zora, smiling.

Coda: How Does It Feel to Be a Problem?

Zora goes her own way. Animated, active, and nonconforming, she
is fearlessly willing to risk punishment in exchange for small moments of fun and social connection. She leveraged disruption, performance, and other strategies of attention-getting to create lively
touches of entertainment and dramatic interludes throughout the
school day. She shined the spotlight on herself during these brief
stints on the classroom's center stage, making herself seen and
heard. Already racially spotlighted as the only child of color in the
class, Zora owned every opportunity to stand out and perform on
her own terms.

Her efforts to be hypervisible, though, resulted in the teachers' equal efforts to make her invisible—to redirect, scold, and train her into fitting in more easily with the others. This response from the school meant she was constantly in trouble. Despite her efforts to deliver a funny and entertaining performance, she was most often cast in the part of troublemaker, assigned to play the role of problematic child of color. In this way, Zora succeeded in being seen, but she was seen as bad. And, importantly, the other young children were an attentive audience, daily receiving the message that being different is a problem, and drawing racial associations.

The consequences Zora bore reminded the other children to attentively toe the line, to blend in rather than stand out. The classroom expectation of assimilation to a prescribed norm was not particular to Zora; it was a value held strongly by the teachers, as Mrs. Norbert and Mrs. Beverly repeatedly used language of wanting the children "not to stand out." When I questioned them about their repeated redirections to Carmen, the anxious child who had a habit of opening her mouth and holding her arms a particular way when speaking publicly, Mrs. Beverly said, "You can't have a person who stands like this with their mouth gaping open." She went on: "She has enough trouble making friends. That's not helping. That's making you stand out in a way, and you have to think down the road about the consequences of standing out like that."

Mrs. Norbert piggybacked: "We talk to them about that. We say, 'Look, if you don't want to stand out, sometimes you have to look more like everyone else. Opening your mouth and sticking your hands out like this, is that going to make you look more like everyone else, or very different?'"

Mrs. Beverly continued: "We had to tell her, 'Right now you're doing these behaviors, especially when you're nervous. But we're going to change those behaviors, because they make you stand out.' You have to try to make them see that they have some choices to make, about how they're going to look to the rest of the world."

This talk of not standing out, not looking different, is strong, consistent, and explicit in the work these teachers do with all their students. They tell the children that making friends, that being seen in a positive way by the "rest of the world," requires that you fit in, not stand out, to be and look and behave like "everyone else."

For Zora, though, this standard was especially difficult and problematic; it was literally impossible for her to look like everyone else. Mrs. Beverly acknowledges the reality of working in a white-bread school, noting that if Zora attended a school populated by more children of color maybe she wouldn't stand out so much. "She wouldn't hear her name as often," she admitted. "She just wouldn't."

But even despite this recognition that context matters, the fact was that Zora was attending *this* school, and there was a certain way to be like everyone else in *this* school. The dominant population— in this case, an overwhelmingly white and affluent one—dictated the norms and standards.

Zora was seeking a sense of belonging, a place of social acceptance and affirmation in her community of peers. Her strategy was to leverage the antics of noncompliance, to stand out, to make herself seen. The teachers wanted Zora to be accepted by her peers, too, but their sense of how children come to belong was in direct conflict with Zora's. Conflating conformity with belonging meant they pushed their continuous desire for acculturation to the mainstream.

Because the teachers believed Zora should change to be more like the majority community, their punitive response to standing out tended to push Zora further to the outskirts of this community. She became a troublemaker in the eyes of her peers, who routinely bore witness to her public reprimands and who were routinely allowed to participate in policing her. The teachers' efforts to make her more acceptable in fact rendered her more and more different—a problematic and troublesome other.

I think of the question W.E.B. DuBois raised more than a century ago: "How does it feel to be a problem?" Of his own boyhood attending school with white children, of his own developing consciousness of difference, he writes, "It dawned upon me with a certain suddenness that I was different from the others; or like, mayhap, in heart and life and longing, but shut out from their world by a vast veil." In the staging of his own difference as a black child in an unwelcoming white space, he speaks of the "double-consciousness" that develops, "this sense of always looking at one's self through the eyes of others, of measuring one's soul by the tape of a world that looks on in amused contempt and pity." [10] While Zora performs her dramatic antics, shining the spotlight of hypervisibility on herself, I wonder how she is coming to see herself through the eyes of her audience, a community of peers who find her simultaneously entertaining and troublesome.

Can Zora love herself through such a gaze?

Whether she is controlled socially through constant redirection or internally through medication, or both, the insistence on making Zora more compliant—more like the others—was required for her success. I worry about her capacity to remain out-standing in light of the persistent demand for sameness.

Lucas

On Being Pigeonholed

The Lucas and The Pigeon

When Lucas Shelton likes something, he really likes it. Not a regular kind of like, but a consuming, fixated, can't-live-without-it kind of like.

That's how he feels about pretty much every children's book written by his favorite author, Mo Willems. But it is especially true of *Don't Let the Pigeon Drive the Bus!*, the first book in Willems's award-winning series about an exasperated pigeon who dreams of and begs for all things that are not allowed. After asking nicely, the smart and eager pigeon attempts clever mind tricks and scheming negotiation tactics: "My cousin Herb drives a bus almost every day! True story."

Or, "Hey, I've got an idea. Let's play 'Drive the Bus'! I'll go first!"

His repeated, failed attempts to win permission generally

culminate in a desperate tantrum. And then, finally, defeated acceptance.

Lucas and this pigeon have a lot in common.

Lucas is with the school-based counselor being tested for special education services. In her office, she has a stuffed Piggie—another character from a Mo Willems collection of books for beginning readers. Lucas immediately spots it and begins the contemplation on how to make it his. As soon as there is a lull in the testing, he asks to play with it. He grabs it from the shelf and starts to act out scenes from the books, which of course he has read many times.

"You've worked very hard today," the psychologist tells him at the end of their session. She offers him a prize from her treasure chest prize box. "Go ahead and pick something."

"I'll take Piggie," Lucas tells her.

"No, Piggie hangs out here with me. He's not one of the choices."

"Fine. Then I want nothing." And he stomps out of the room, slamming the door behind him.

When the story gets reported to his teacher, Mrs. Norbert, she sees an opportunity to help Lucas understand that his response was inappropriate. "I'm like, that's not a way to behave, and I made him go back and apologize."

The next day, he returns to the office for the next session of testing—aware that his previous strategy for winning Piggie failed. He is ready with his plan, and lays in with the Piggie business right away. "I was thinking," he begins. "I know Piggie belongs to you, but maybe I could just have him over to my house for a playdate."

The creative negotiations begin.

When that offer fails, he resorts to answering all the psychologist's questions in a Piggie voice. Pretending is a strategy that helps him meet the urgency of his needs in the absence of formal permission. Maybe he can't own Piggie, but Piggie can still live inside him.

While starting to get to know Lucas, I serendipitously heard an interview with Mo Willems on National Public Radio. He is hilarious, and the interview is every bit as entertaining as his books. "So tell me about the Pigeon," says the interviewer. "He's just so much desire and so much frustration."

"He's The Pigeon," Willems replies. "The fact is his first name is 'The.' That should tell you enough about who he is and where he thinks his place in the world is."

Yes, I think. The Pigeon and The Lucas have a lot in common.

Sharing Space

Lucas's place in the world began in utero, sharing space with his fraternal twin brother. I am talking with his mother, Corinne, as she recounts these earliest beginnings. "In all the ultrasounds, Lucas was the active baby," she says. "He was right there. Easy to find. Toby was so quiet that sometimes we couldn't even find him." She goes on to tell me that Toby developed torticollis, a condition in which the head and neck are abnormally twisted or rotated because of the position of the two fetuses in the womb. "Whatever position they were in, Lucas was sitting on him. He was sitting on his brother's neck. So that kind of tells the tale right there."

We are on the sofa in her living room, and Toby is hovering nearby as she explains. He is curious about my presence and likes to hear her stories. Lucas, on the other hand, is in the basement playing—enjoying his relative freedom while mom is tied up with me.

"I have to say," Corinne continues, "that Toby was the one with more problems in the beginning. He had the torticollis, he had pyloric stenosis—which is a blockage of the intestines—so he had surgery at six weeks. He did physical therapy. He had an allergic reaction to something. So Lucas was kind of the easy baby for the first two years, and then it switched. For the first two years he was pretty mellow. He used to be a great sleeper—"

Toby interrupts her. "Was I the bad sleeper?"

"Yeah," she replies. "But now you're the good sleeper, so it doesn't make any sense, does it?"

"Now Lucas is the bad sleeper," says Toby.

"He has trouble sleeping?" I ask.

"Yeah," answers Toby, before mom gets the chance. They share a bedroom, so he would know.

"He used to be a solid sleeper. Toby was the tough one. Everything was Toby. He was the fussier one and Lucas was mellow. And Lucas walked, talked, and crawled faster than Toby. In fact, I even took Toby to see an orthopedist because I was worried about him not walking. When we got there and the doctor saw Lucas toddling around, he said, 'You're here for the wrong baby.' Something was wrong with Lucas's hips, so the doctor ended up examining both of them. By age two, it seemed like everything switched. Toby's problems panned out, and then Lucas—Lucas got ear tubes, which his sister also had. He became more noise sensitive, and he developed asthma. I feel like that's where it all began."

We had started by talking about Lucas, of course, but it struck me how Corinne described him largely in conversation with his brother. As they are twins, memories of the one are intertwined with memories of the other, and comparisons between them seem natural since they arrived in the world at the same time. These comparisons continue, as Toby has a much easier time at school than Lucas.

Corinne easily recalled and recounted the multiple physical needs and conditions of both boys in those earliest months and years: reflux, allergies, torticollis, the hips. By toddlerhood, both Toby and Lucas were regulars at multiple doctors' offices— pediatricians and physical therapists and orthopedists and on and on. "You must have been exhausted," I say to her, imagining what it was like to trek three tiny children all around the city to so many appointments.

It is easy to imagine Corinne doing all this shuttling, because even now, I often watch her running between her three children's classrooms on the many special occasions hosted by Forest School. She is a regular presence, and the secretaries and principal know her by name and chat her up during visits. I never failed to see Corinne, a more-than-full-time mother, at a school event, and I rarely went a week without running into her in the school building. Her husband had a particularly demanding work schedule, which prevented him from attending most of these events, and Corinne bore the heavy weight of responsibility for all things school related—from breakfast in the morning to lunch preparation to homework and after-school activities to bedtime routines.

The medical focus of her efforts, too, continued, as she fought for all three of her children to be evaluated for special education services and interventions. Straightforward and evaluative language of strengths and shortcomings—good sleepers versus bad, fussy babies versus mellow, difficult kids versus easy—were commonplace in her descriptions of her own children and fit well with the school's similar approach to describing students. Because I was talking with her as someone interested in Lucas's behavior at school, these were the kinds of descriptions that seemed appropriate to her for our discussions. And they were the kinds of descriptions she was used to having to provide; she had grown to be something of an expert on all the requisite behavioral terminology. By this point she had filled out countless evaluation forms for each of her three children, in the offices of doctors and other medical specialists, in parent-teacher conferences, in special education evaluations and meetings. She is well trained in talking about her children through diagnostic lenses.

In Corinne's home, though, she displays a different and much more full picture of her children than these initial medical descriptions and evaluations suggest. The living room walls are covered with framed photographs of the family, while mantels and side tables hold many more of these images. In them I can see the children grow from birth to the present—wide smiles, tight hugs, special occasions preserved in these many still images. They are deeply human images that show these little ones outside of the role of student, celebrating the children as brothers and sister, sons and daughter, cherished and wonderfully spoiled grandchildren.

And the children themselves force reminders of their human being. When I ask Corinne about whether she can recall any lasting memories of Lucas's baby years, she repeats that he was a "good baby" no sooner than she is interrupted with another of Toby's interjections.

"He was a cute baby!" he says, laughing, and drawing a laugh from us. "He was, though!" This seems to draw Corinne's attention away from the evaluation and toward more open description.

"He was. You can see him here," she says, motioning to the photos that surround us. "He was happy. Such a happy baby. And goofy. He's always been so goofy." She smiles.

Though the Shelton home is large, it is strikingly cozy—with warm colors and many shared spaces where the family gathers. The boys share a room that is well stocked with books and decorations and toys, and I see all of Lucas's favorite characters featured: Piggie, Sonic the Hedgehog, some old plush *Blues Clues* toys from a previous phase of his perseveration. Some of the children's artwork was framed and hung, and the basement served as another place for play and gathering. It was large enough for all the children to play together and was similarly stocked with various forms of entertainment. During my visit all three of the children spent hours down there together, uninterrupted and without need of mediation, redirection, or discipline.

Both at school and at home, Corinne regularly showered all three of her children with much physical affection. When she visited Mrs. Norbert's classroom Lucas never hesitated to rush over to her for a hug and to receive some kisses on the top of his head. Even their tiny dog—which I imagined to be gigantic based on the bark I could hear from the driveway upon my arrival—sat snuggled and curled up on Corinne's lap the entire time we talked. She was caring for many small living things in that house, and her love for them was abundant.

Corinne's philosophies and ways of being as a parent were closely aligned with the values emphasized by Mrs. Norbert and within Forest School more generally—particularly the need for strictly enforced rules and limits on behavior. Lucas had attended a small, local lab preschool in which children were afforded many freedoms and much space to be who they were, and Corinne lamented their approach. "Sometimes they just needed to say, *That is not acceptable*, boom, that's it. Lucas could have benefited from that."

Though Corinne can easily name and explain Lucas's personal, individual, and medical struggles, while recounting his kindergarten experience—the year before he joined Mrs. Norbert's class—she simultaneously identifies some of the contextual factors that impeded his success at school. That year, Forest had miscalculated their kindergarten enrollment and ended up with unfortunately large class sizes. She explains how difficult it was for Lucas to share such a crowded space: "It was twenty-six, twenty-seven kids in the class that year. Even with two adults that's still more than twelve kids a teacher to monitor, and there were quite a few kids in that class with problems. . . . Lucas had problems on the bus; he had problems in the classroom. He didn't want to go. He didn't like it. It was too crowded. I think it was just too much for him. It was too stimulating, too overwhelming, too much. I felt like it was too much. I think you're learning how to be in a kindergarten class, and learning how to follow the rules, and all that, and then when you have attention issues on top of that, on top of twenty-seven kids, on top of many other kids in there with problems—it was all too much. Especially for a kindergarten classroom. It's too important because kids are trying to learn how to be in school."

From the start of his life in the womb, Lucas learned to compete for resources in a small, shared space, and to go after his own needs in an effort to thrive. Learning "how to be in school" would require much training—an education in how to thrive without sitting on anyone else's neck.

Just as The Pigeon declares the existence of his "dream" of driving the bus, Lucas devotes much time and energy to disrupting the rules of school in order to assert his own wishes and desires. Lucas would have to learn to measure his own needs and preferences—which he experienced as particularly pressing and urgent—against the requirements and demands of everyday, shared classroom life.

He would have to learn school.

Learning School

It is early September. The children in Mrs. Norbert's class gather on the rug for a read-aloud. Lucas, a first grader, is sitting in shorts with his pale, white, skinny legs folded. He sits as close to the front as is both possible and allowed. He is practically sitting on the teacher's feet.

Eagerly awaiting the start, his wide blue eyes are intently focused on the book despite the distraction of his blond hair constantly tickling his eyelashes. Fall allergies have started to take their toll, so a steady stream is leaking from his nose. It doesn't seem to bother him.

He's wearing his Sonic the Hedgehog T-shirt today. It reads, "This is what awesome looks like."

As he grows impatient with waiting he begins to obsess over a spot on the leg of his shorts. "Be gone, spot" he says with his characteristic lisp, and he tries to rub it out. The longer the story is taking to begin, the more the spot is bothering him. After about two minutes, which seems to Lucas an unbearable eternity, Mrs. Norbert begins to read.

Shortly, though, Lucas decides that this book, on this day, is not for him. His body starts to wiggle and his attention once again shifts to the spot on his shorts. "You are the stubbornest spot on the face of the planet," he mumbles playfully. "But one day I. Will. Conquer. You. Mwah-ha-ha-ha." His rendition of the evil laugh is superb, and his goofiness and talent for performance are shining through. He smiles to himself.

He begins to look around the room. This often happens when he is called to the rug for whole-group lessons, where his attention quickly wanes. His eyes move to the ceiling, the back wall, the door. He's taking in the calendar, the Lego bricks, the stuffed puppets. Sometimes he mouths silently as he reads things around the room. Finally, his eyes settle on the classroom library at the back corner. He stands up and begins to inconveniently and disruptively climb over the other children to leave the rug area. Mrs. Norbert looks at him but continues her reading. She probably assumes he has a legitimate reason for leaving—perhaps to grab a tissue. Lucas goes over to the library, chooses *Henny Penny* after rifling through several book boxes, returns to the rug, and begins to flip the pages.

"What are you doing, Lucas?" Mrs. Norbert's tone is one of disbelief.

"Well," he replies, matter-of-fact, "I wanted to look at a book." He doesn't seem to get what all the fuss is all about.

"No! You don't decide that! When I'm reading a book, you're listening."

Sulking, pouting, he puts the book away.

We talk about the incident months later. "There's a lot of that," Mrs. Norbert tells me. "He's like, *Carry on, Mrs. Norbert. I'm just going to do my own thing.*" She laughs. "That's where I'm like, I can't believe this kid has had full-day kindergarten. He has picked up no school culture at all." School culture dictates that he follow the directives of The Teacher, not The Lucas.

Mrs. Beverly chimes in: "Nobody has bothered to fight the fight with him. We would have fought that fight in kindergarten. You're fighting it now. And you're winning, Jane," she says approvingly to her co-teacher.

To "fight the fight" is to insist, in spite of a child's protest, on upholding the rules of school—the "culture." Watching Lucas simply get up and leave the rug area shocks me as an observer. How dare he? I am well enough versed in the culture of schooling to know this is far from acceptable. But when he seems surprised by being called out, he forces me to consider how much he is already presumed to understand. It all suddenly feels complicated. He is supposed to know that getting up for a tissue would be okay, but getting up for a book is not. He is supposed to know that his choice of book is superseded by the teacher's, at this particular moment in the school day. He is supposed to know that the teacher is not to be interrupted with his questions or reactions, though she will interrupt herself to ask the children questions she deems useful and appropriate. There is so much to understand, much of it quite subtle, but the others—despite their very young age—already seem to get it.

On many occasions I hear him lament, after being redirected, "I can't do *anything* around here."

He is learning school.

———

For a child like Lucas, who experiences most of his own interests as urgent, internalizing and adapting to school culture is no easy feat. Rules don't seem fair because they often stand in the way of meeting his individual desires. Rules exist to maintain order and sanity in a room full of more than twenty children, and they are designed to prioritize the mass—not the individual and his own preferences.

But Lucas is a child for whom individual desire is exceptionally strong. He is inflexible and perseverating; it's just his nature. Mrs. Norbert often uses the word *egocentric* to describe him. "I don't mean conceited," she explains. "I mean it literally. He can't think outside of himself. In his mind, the world outside him doesn't exist." She offers an example of how his egocentrism plays out: "He did something, I don't even remember what, and he lost five minutes of recess. And so he was mad about that, or unhappy. He wasn't angry, but he didn't like it. So I said, 'Well, why don't you think about that? If someone did that to you, would you like that?'

"And he said, 'No.'

"And I said, 'Do you think that they should miss some recess?'

"And he said, 'Yes.'

"'So, can you understand why you're missing some recess?'

"'No. Because I don't want to miss recess.'"

I can't help but find this funny, and we both laugh—though I'm guessing she did not laugh at the time. It does sound true to Lucas. It is indeed difficult for him to step out of himself, even as he can clearly understand fairness from an objective standpoint. He knows what would be fair in this situation, but that doesn't translate into his ability to accept the consequence as fair to *him*.

Her story reminded me of a similar situation I had witnessed. Lucas kicked a child out of frustration after some kind of altercation, and an empathetic approach was again used to try to help him understand his infraction. "Would you like to be kicked?" the adult asked. She was the paraprofessional tasked with watching the children at recess, and she often ended up talking children through their interactions with one another.

"No, of course not," Lucas replies.

"So is it fair to kick someone else?"

"Yes, if they deserve it."

The paraprofessional is getting frustrated, but she persists. "If you deserved it, should *you* be kicked?"

"I already answered that. No. But we're not talking about me right now. Can we focus, please?" She is disarmed by Lucas's unintentional humor.

Relationships are difficult because his tendency is to meet his own needs—to sit on other people's necks. One time, when he actively and enthusiastically crushes another child's Lego creation with his plastic dinosaur toy, Mrs. Norbert furiously demands an explanation.

"Why, Lucas?!"

"Because. My dinosaur needed something to attack."

Similarly, on another occasion when we are all outside for field day and Lucas's class is having to wait quite some time for the other competitions to finish up, his attention is drawn to a pattern he notices on a nearby tree trunk that looks somewhat like a target. He picks up a stone and hurls it, aiming for the center. But a child is standing right there, directly in the path of his toss, and he truly seems to fail to see her at all. The stone misses her by a long shot thanks to his poor aim, but she becomes livid just the same. "Oops, I didn't see you," he says, simply and straightforwardly. "You should move over, because you're right in the way of my bull's-eye." He really does perceive her to be in his way.

Needless to say, this doesn't do much for his relationships. His mother worries about his social skills: "Sometimes he goes off into his crazy little games, and other kids aren't interested in that, and that's where he doesn't know how to shut it off. He doesn't know how to say, *Oh, okay, well, what would you want to do?*, where somebody else might stop and say, *Okay, well if you don't want to play that, what do you want to play?* He just walks away."

Compromise is difficult for an inflexible child, and he often prioritizes his choice of an activity over a social relationship. But he doesn't understand the situation in these terms; instead, he feels that if the other child doesn't share his interest in a particular activity, then that child is rejecting him. This proves very upsetting to him.

Corinne tells me that Lucas is the same way in his relationship with his sister, Lucy. As Lucy gets older and is hitting the preteen years, she's increasingly less interested in the kinds of things Lucas and his brother like. She plays with him less and less, and Lucas's sensitivity is triggered so that he blows up at her. "I try to explain that Lucy is getting older so she just doesn't like the same activities anymore," Corinne says. But Lucas interprets the situation through his own needs rather than Lucy's changing needs, and he takes it personally. "I feel angry that Lucy is getting older," he tells me.

"See?" says his mother. "He gets mad at her because she won't do what he wants. He thinks she doesn't care about him anymore."

Lucas's egocentrism can be mistaken for selfishness, or can make him seem unsympathetic. But, to the contrary, his extremely high level of sensitivity and overreaction allows him to demonstrate deep care and thoughtfulness—albeit in his own quirky way.

During the school year, Lucas's maternal grandmother became very ill. Lucas and his family were very close to her and it was a difficult and painful time for all. Although Lucas could not tolerate the trips to the nursing home, his brother and older sister were better able to bear the visits. When she died and the whole family was grieving, Lucas was the one to notice and acknowledge his mother's particular and acute pain. "He's very observant," she says, "though you wouldn't expect it because he always seems like he's distracted and running around." She continues: "[At the hospital] the other two—his sister cried, his brother said nothing, but Lucas actually said something to my mom, like that he was sorry she was upset. And [when she died] he told me—What did he say? Oh, he says to me that the sooner I can accept the circle of life, the better." She laughs, even as tears have welled up in her eyes. Though Lucas uses a not-so-gentle approach here—an approach that actually might be quite effective with *him* because he is matter-of-fact and no-nonsense—he is trying to reach out to comfort his mother as well as he knows how.

"I'm like, okay, thanks. This isn't a nature movie, buddy. But he lectured me on how we had a great ninety-seven years. He just, he comes out and says things you don't expect, that are insightful. He was trying. He was the only one that said anything [to comfort me]. So I think the sympathy, the empathy is there."

I witness his care firsthand on the playground one day when Lucas hurts another child during a game of tag. He's just too hyper and overexcited, and this results in an accidental roughness that causes a slight injury. While the other children rush over to tattle on him, Lucas is sitting at the crying boy's side, rubbing his back. "Are you okay, buddy? I'm really sorry." Rather than hustle over to defend himself against the rushing accusers, he focuses his attention on making amends and providing comfort.

Lucas is definitely interested in relationships, and certainly has the capacity for empathy. But he is learning to balance the needs of others against the urgency of his own. This, too, is an important part of learning school—learning not just what will get him in trouble with teachers, but also what will get him in trouble with his peers.

Performing Belonging

VROOM-VROOM
VROOMY
VROOM-VROOM!

Despite the challenges he faces with relationships, I see Lucas make many creative social attempts, and his humor is a powerful tool in winning the affection of adults and children alike. He is bold in using that tool, largely because he doesn't seem to have the filter of self-consciousness or even self-reflection. During a play the children performed for parents, for example, when the audience applauds too early, he is the child who confidently and unabashedly goes off script to say, loudly, "It's not over. You need to hold your applause, folks." His interjections were more entertaining than the performance itself.

Similarly, when Mrs. Norbert is rushing him to join the line he is holding up, making all the children late to art, he says surreptitiously to the child next to him, "Man alive. It's like she thinks I'm Sonic. I can't just activate my jets." His rich vocabulary and literary skill, indisputably complex for a six-year-old, make his clever humor all the more enjoyable.

Being an entertainer—both by accident and on purpose—is a strategy he draws on often, even as it gets him into trouble. On these occasions his desire for belonging and social approval seems to outweigh the risk of punishment.

While working in stations during a Native American unit of study, the children are collaborating in a small group to construct a poster after watching a video of music-making by an indigenous leader. Before the video started, Lucas had done some kind of rap performance for the group and gotten their laughs and approval.

This makes him want to continue his antics. The kids are sharing a very small space because they all have to gather around a tiny computer screen. One of the girls is getting extremely annoyed with Lucas because he's disruptive during the viewing. He moves his body too much, he covers his ears, he makes jokes and sings along loudly, he drums on the table. The girl repeatedly tries to regulate him. Another girl gives the two-finger quiet signal right in his face.

He is talking aloud during the entire video. Finally, one of the boys reprimands him, too. But Lucas is also pretty funny and quite entertaining, so the kids are laughing, and they oscillate between policing him and encouraging him. "I had no idea you were this funny, Lucas!" says one of the little girls. He looks absolutely pleased with himself.

But I can tell things are ramping up because it's just too small a space to share with this kind of behavior. He's making increasingly dramatic motions and someone is bound to get hurt. When it's time to transition to the poster, Lucas can't let go of his funny business. Having received so much social approval, he was not about to quit. The boys are really urging him on now, while the girls try to work on the poster on their own. Finally, furious, one of the girls complains to Mrs. Norbert and Lucas is publicly and sternly reprimanded.

Though he sometimes cries when redirected so harshly, on this occasion he seems nonplussed. Mostly he seems quite happy.

Still, though, the approval of the other children is conditional, and they sold him out when it came time. The other boys, who had been egging him on and did nothing to contribute to the poster, did not stand by him when the consequence was being handed down, nor did they take any shared responsibility. His relationships are uneven and sometimes unfair. "Even at recess," Mrs. Norbert explains, "the other boys sometimes abuse him. They tag him, because he's the slowest runner. He can never catch them, and they don't want to tag their cool friends."

"They use him," adds Mrs. Beverly. "He's being used."

But Lucas reports to me that recess is his favorite time of the day. "It's so fun. That's my happiest." He does not perceive the unfairness we adults identify. To play with the others despite his objectively subordinate role is satisfying his need for a sense of belonging, a space of friendship.

Exasperation

Yet, when Lucas *does* perceive unfairness, watch out. The inability to control others' interactions with him is often the cause of significant perseveration. Lucas's extreme level of frustration leads to exasperation and can make for a volatile set of exchanges and a lot of reprimands. This, too, makes peer relationships difficult.

As in the incident with the poster, when the children work in small groups, Lucas often messes around and does what he wants—sometimes trying to entertain the others—rather than focusing on the task at hand. On one occasion when the children are debriefing their group work as a whole class, a member of Lucas's small group—a popular and revered boy—begins a not-so-subtle callout. "Well, *one* of our group members was not really paying attention, and it was annoying." His eyes dart in Lucas's direction, and everyone knows just exactly what is going on here.

Lucas's face changes immediately. He gets red, and his eyes go from wide, bright circles to angry, thin slits. He is shooting venom from them, glaring at the boy. "You'll pay for that," he mumbles under his breath. The teacher tells Lucas to fix his face and encourages the other child to continue. The child is (appropriately) hesitant to carry on with his evaluation.

"Because now he fears for his life!" Mrs. Norbert reports to me with a laugh. Lucas was stewing over the incident for several hours. His hurt at being embarrassed and made hypervisible by the popular boy's negative assessment resulted in an angry inability to let it go.

Lucas spends nearly all of his social time with a pair of other children—Sam and Stella—who are always together as a twosome. Stella and Lucas often compete for Sam's attention and friendship because Sam is fairly easy to control. He's a happy-go-lucky kid who simply doesn't have strong preferences of his own. "Two bosses and one follower," says Mrs. Norbert. "Of course that's going to turn into a competition."

Stella is a clever little girl who knows exactly how to push Lucas's buttons in order to win alone time with Sam. When the three of them are looking at a *Where's Waldo?* book at lunchtime, where the task is to spot the character of Waldo on an incredibly dense and busy page of drawing, Stella pretends to find him. "Here he is!" She points to someone who is clearly not Waldo. She looks at Lucas in eager and intended anticipation of his exasperation. She wants him to get mad because she knows he gets out of control and into big trouble when he's mad. Then she and Sam can have the book to themselves.

"That's *not* Waldo and you know it, Stella. Don't be ridiculous." His lisp is stronger when he's upset.

"It is!"

"Of course it isn't. This guy has a blue hat. Waldo does not have a blue hat." His voice is rising, his cheeks reddening.

"I have been doing this a lot longer than you have, Lucas! You are just getting started in this! I know what I am talking about. This is him! Turn the page."

Lucas's face turns so red that I half expect steam to rise from his ears. The incident ends with him grabbing the book from her hands, scratching her in the process, and throwing it on the ground. He then gets in trouble and loses several minutes of recess.

Knowing his proclivity for exasperation, Stella preys on him by exploiting this weakness. He can't resist engaging, and he can't let it go. It isn't Waldo and he will insist on that despite the consequences.

Similarly, while researching diamondback rattlesnakes, Lucas watches a short video in class put out by the Discovery Channel about desert animals. The video shows a scene of a roadrunner pecking at a rattlesnake enough to conquer it. Lucas is incensed. "*Not* possible. That would *never* happen. The snake would run away. The snake would win if it was snake versus roadrunner. This is crazy." Mrs. Norbert reasons with him, using the logic explained in the video. He gets more and more riled up, and the perseveration ensues. "Not possible," he mumbles repeatedly to himself. "Ridiculous." Mrs. Norbert tells him to let it go, which is asking the impossible. Minutes later, hours later, even the next day, Lucas is still talking about the ridiculousness of that video. It offends him to the core.

He similarly experiences offense—personal offense—when he perceives that a rule has been broken by a peer. One day in the lunchroom, when for some reason the cafeteria is more crowded than usual, two children from another class join his table. This is extremely upsetting to Lucas. He begins to question and police them. *Why are you here? What do you want? This is a table for Mrs. Norbert's class. Only Mrs. Norbert's kids are allowed to sit here. Whose class are you in? What happened to your table?* None of the other children seem affected by the newcomers. The more time passes without the boys leaving the table, the more Lucas is obsessing over the perceived inappropriateness of their barging in. The redness in his face starts up, and he is getting increasingly angry. I watch him ramp up as he begins to mumble about wanting them gone. He gets up and starts kicking the garbage can, hard. The children look to me.

"Why, Lucas?" I ask.

"It's not fair. There are rules. The rule is that this table is only for Mrs. Norbert's kids. They're not following the rules and nobody is doing anything about it." At this point in the year Lucas has learned school culture, by hard training, and it has been a painful series of lessons. No transgression will go unpunished, because his never do.

"I think they're here because there isn't room for them at their own tables," I attempt to explain. "That doesn't seem fair, either. Everyone should have a place to eat lunch, right?"

"Yes, obviously. Just not at this table."

He couldn't bear the intrusion. Rules are rules. And if he has to follow them, so does everyone else—to the letter and without exception. "He's the fair police," says Mrs. Norbert. He simply could not let it go. Ultimately he chose to move to another table rather than sit with the interlopers.

Exasperation is the result of Lucas being all desire and frustration, and he is most often in trouble because his exasperation causes him to behave unacceptably. As the year goes on, however, he learns some creative ways to meet his needs despite the demands of school culture.

Some strategies are more creative than others. During a math lesson he tries a more direct approach: "Don't you think we've wasted enough time on this?" He stands up and announces the question just as the lesson is beginning. Mrs. Beverly is teaching on this occasion, and her wit allows a quick retort: "Oh, you're measuring time. That's a math skill, you know."

"Okay, very funny," says Lucas. "But really, I think we can all agree that we've spent enough time on this." His tone is not aggressive. It's just matter-of-fact. As compared to throwing a tantrum, this approach is more within the realm of reasonable. It's a negotiation attempt rather than immediate overreaction. And though it is still inappropriate, his unintentional humor again saves him.

"I just couldn't help but crack up," says Mrs. Beverly.

Acceptance

By the end of my time with Lucas, as first grade comes to a close, I see that he has learned to accept much of what is required by school. Sometimes he is too frustrated to cope and ends up exploding and receiving a reprimand, and he does continue to hone his negotiation skills and develop his repertoire of escape strategies. But for the most part, the teachers "fought the fight" and won.

To understand his own view of the demands of school life, I asked him to complete a few sentence prompts. He responded in these ways, where the italicized text are his words:

Rule number one: You'll get in trouble if *you don't listen.*

You will definitely get in trouble if *you're too slow.*

When you're at school, don't think about *anything besides learning.*

It seems to me he is absorbing school culture. By and large, outside of choice time, it isn't a place for individual desires, thoughts, or distractions. It's a time to listen, to focus, to be quick, to concentrate on nothing "besides learning."

Sometimes he beats Mrs. Norbert to the punch when she is about to reprimand and redirect him. "I know, I know, I know . . . ," he is often heard saying. When his writing folder is bursting at the seams, papers flying out of it right and left, Mrs. Norbert hardly opens her mouth before he interrupts, "Yes, I know, I know. I have too much things." He grabs the unruly stack of pages and sticks them into his backpack.

When she leaves the room for a moment and he sees an opportunity for freedom, he immediately trades his assigned task for a chance to read a book of choice from the library. He looks around to make sure she hasn't returned. But then he becomes so engrossed in the book that he fails to notice when she has in fact returned. And, of course, she doesn't miss a beat. As soon as he notices her hovering over him: "I know, I know, I know. I'll finish. Don't worry. Here I go." And he returns to the required task.

I notice that he can increasingly attend to the needs of his peers, too, as the year progresses. "If you had to live on the moon with just one friend, who would you pick?" I ask.

"Sam and Stella," he replies, even though Stella's constant conflict with him is well documented.

"Both?" I ask, to be sure.

"Yeah. They love each other." This strikes me as a particular and beautiful reflection of his ability to show both care and empathy. He understands that they are a pair, even if he would rather that were not the case. Being friends with Sam means accepting the reality of Stella.

Lucas is already working on himself to better share space and learn school. Much of this is driven by the demands of the other children themselves, rather than Mrs. Norbert's imperatives. With Stella, for example, it was another child in the class—Jeffrey—who helped Lucas understand the dynamic of sharing a friend and coming to grips with it. At lunch after a particularly vicious fight with Stella, after Sam tries to mediate the initial conflict, Jeffrey writes a note. It is titled, *Lucas, Stella wants to be your friend.* This is not necessarily true, but Lucas was the one enraged so the boy thought to start with him. The note read:

> Just say these words:
> "I want to be your friend."
> Why?
> Because if you don't you guys will argue a lot.

Here we see how children, too, sometimes work on teaching one another school—educating one another about how to share space. As in this example, their attempts were often less punitive than a teacher's. Their attempts were softer, more explanatory. Here the boy uses coaching, literally giving Lucas some language he can use. And he takes the time to explain why Lucas should give it a try.

Fundamentally, though, Lucas would always have just a little extra trouble learning school. "He just is who he is," says his mother. "It's an internal issue. It's not a situationally driven thing." She locates the problem in his body, and she feels that he needs to be the one to adapt to the reality of what is required. "He needs to be more flexible. Sometimes he's just his own worst enemy."

On the one hand, I agree that Lucas needs to do all he can to be flexible, to adapt to collective and community needs. On the other hand, school is a place in which there is an incredibly high demand to be obedient and to reject one's own desires in favor of what is required. Lucas may be particularly ill suited for such a context, it's true, but in a non-school context where there is more freedom and autonomy, his "internal" issues would not show themselves so starkly. In this way, his extreme inability to cope is situational—the situation of school, and the culture of obedience, conformity, rules, and requirements.

Lucas is active, energetic, unruly, imaginative. Those characteristics are problematic in spaces that require sitting still, listening attentively, following rules, being realistic. He is working on changing himself to adapt to the demands of school. He is working on accepting things, on becoming *less* Lucas. I can't help but admire his efforts to *stay* Lucas—to negotiate, to creatively skirt, to pretend, to sneak around a bit. As a teacher I might find it infuriating, but as an observer and a person, I find it clever and creative. I find him positively lovable.

Mrs. Norbert and Mrs. Beverly, too, can't help but enjoy him. "He's hysterical," they both agree. "I can't help but love him," says Mrs. Norbert. "I absolutely love having him in my class."

Coda: Don't Pigeonhole Me

Sometimes everyone—his mother, his teachers, his specialists—took for granted that they knew Lucas well because he was so predictable so much of the time. This prompted people to pigeonhole him. When the children wrote several poems and had to choose one for a public poetry reading, Lucas was debating which to select. "It's a five-way tie right now," he tells me.

In this moment he was, in true form, hastily illustrating his poem titled "Soccer":

> I *play soccer*
> I *don't give up*
> *When I fall*
> I *get back up.*

"That's a solid poem," I say. "Maybe you should share it."

He nods, considering.

But when Mrs. Norbert is preparing the program and having the children make their final selections, she comes to Lucas's name and says, "The Sonic poem, Lucas?"

"Yep," he replies, and I wonder how that five-way tie got settled so quickly in his mind.

I, too, pigeonholed him. I caught myself doing this when I made some paper Sonic characters to use in our interview. Mostly I used these as a way to motivate him to cooperate with my request for his insights. I thought he would require some kind of persuasion, and I preyed on his known interest. But to my surprise, he needed no convincing: "Okay, let's do this thing," he said as I took him away from play for our interview. "Tell me all the things you want to know," he offered generously. And he settled into a long-haul sitting position, arms folded behind his head, leaning back against his bed—ready to be patient.

Again to my surprise, I underestimated him once more when I told him he could keep the characters when we were done, and he read the action as a gift. "You made these just for me?" He beamed. "Oh my gosh, thank you! You really care about me because you know I love Sonic! I can't believe I can have these. Thank you so much! I'm going to hang them up. These are wonderful." He was so sweet and so gracious, so genuinely thankful. In point of fact I was not being caring when I made the characters—I was being egocentric, motivated by my own needs. I required his cooperation and I was trying, in a mild way, to coerce his participation by engaging a known interest of his. But Lucas assumed the best of me, and he humbled me. I had underestimated his capacity for *not* pigeonholing others, for being more open and generous in his evaluations and assumptions.

By the end of kindergarten, Lucas was pegged as a problem— pigeonholed as distractible, inflexible, impatient, egocentric, perseverating. He had already started medication for ADHD. His parents felt the pills were helping him and were not hesitant to try them out. His mother, especially, felt that other parents often worked hard to insist on their children's perfection, and she experienced empowerment when she could understand Lucas's conditions and respond to them proactively and with the help of medical doctors and his teachers.

Unlike Zora's parents, who openly encourage standing out, Lucas's parents were on board with the school's effort to train him to fit in. "His preschool was a little too *kumbaya*," his mother says. "They accepted everything and everyone. He could have benefited earlier from some intervention, and from the kind of firm redirection Mrs. Norbert gives him. She and I are much more in sync."

They are also in sync on the topic of medication, which Mrs. Norbert said she "would not want to see him without." By the end of first grade, his mother was looking to increase the dosage of ADHD medication and Lucas was tested for special education services. He was all over the map in terms of his scores and scales, sometimes even testing on the autism and Asperger's spectrums. His results made pigeonholing him impossible. But like both his sister and his brother, he acquired an IEP—an individualized education program that serves as a contract between the school district and a family. "I feel like now I have the legal backing to make sure the accommodations he needs are there," his mother told me. Both she and Mrs. Norbert felt he was well on his way to greater gains in second grade.

I nevertheless found myself wishing for a more contextual and nuanced understanding of his behaviors. Certainly Lucas has a particular nature. His strong desire to meet his own needs over the needs of others seemed to begin before he even officially entered the world, sitting on his twin brother in utero. But the everyday life of classrooms undoubtedly exacerbated his more challenging qualities, bringing them into stark relief. I think of Philip Jackson's classic 1968 study, *Life in Classrooms*, specifically his descriptions of the "hidden curriculum" children are required to learn when they enter school. Despite the age of Jackson's work, the highly stable reality of schools makes his description as apt now as it was decades ago. He summarizes one of the fundamental parts of this hidden curriculum, this requirement that children learn the norms of school—what Mrs. Norbert and Mrs. Beverly called, simply, "school culture." Jackson identifies an aspect of this curriculum that Lucas will undoubtedly have particular trouble mastering, the requirement to follow the needs of the teacher over the preferences of The Lucas:

> [One] view of the teacher's authority might focus on the process of substitution by which the teacher's plans for action are substituted for the student's own. When students do what the teacher tells them to do they are, in effect, abandoning one set of plans (their own) in favor of another (their teacher's). At times, of course, these two sets of plans do not conflict and may even be quite similar. But at other times that which is given up in no way resembles the action called for by the teacher. The lack of resemblance must partially account for the difficulty some students have in adjusting to the classroom. . . . The important point is that students must learn to employ their executive powers in the service of the teacher's desires rather than their own. Even if it hurts.[11]

When Lucas boldly chooses *Henny Penny* over the book the teacher is reading aloud, he disrupts the norm of choosing the teacher's preference over his own, and she has to teach him that *"No!* You don't decide that." This most basic requirement of school—trading your own desires for the requirements of the teacher—may be part of a "hidden curriculum," but Lucas makes it quite visible in his transgressions and often displays his hurt through anger and frustration.

Similarly, Jackson provides a theoretical understanding of Lucas's difficulty sharing space. He names four key features of school life: delay, denial, interruption, and social distraction. And he writes, "Each is produced, in part, by the crowded conditions of the classroom." [12] These four features require that children— even very young children, whom we know to be active and impatient—wait a whole lot, get denied the choice of their own work, get interrupted from their own play, and become distracted by the requirement to be with others socially only at "appropriate" and designated times. These are all normalized school demands and they are largely considered unproblematic, even as we make such demands of five- and six-year-olds, whom we know to be naturally unsuited to them. The fact that the demands are considered normal makes them hidden, part of a neutral and unproblematic school culture. This invisibility draws us to the conclusion that classroom life is regular and children who don't comply with it are irregular. Thus we rely on changing children rather than changing classroom demands.

Children like Lucas, with their exasperation and perseverating insistence on their own desires, their angry red faces and blowups, remind us that our demands are not neutral but, rather, quite challenging and potentially even toxic to the ability of young children to be themselves. Still, these hidden norms prevail, as normal now as they were in 1968, and children today are still evaluated based on how well they meet the standardized requirements of classroom life.

As part of the children's end-of-year portfolios, they are asked to draw trees. Mrs. Norbert and Mrs. Beverly call the task "A Tale of Two Trees" and offer families the following preface to the two drawings:

> Your child's artwork is more than just making pretty pictures. It shows maturity and growth in their reasoning ability. This is why we have the children draw the tree more than once.
>
> The first tree, done at the beginning of the year, is often a "lollipop" tree with a ball of green for leaves and a straight trunk. There may be a hole for a squirrel or apples on the tree. Occasionally, children will represent the tree with a strip of sky and ground as their background. They see this as the "correct" way of showing the horizon. In these pictures, the sun is generally in the corner with rays radiating out. A next level would be to have the sky meet the ground.
>
> The second tree, done at the end of the year, is usually a more realistic representation. Branches now are crooked, leaves have shape and definition. Roots can be showing and bark may have texture. Colors are typically blended to be more accurate.
>
> Children start to take more risks to represent the world they see with their eyes versus that which they imagine in their minds. They replace what they think things look like with a more accurate version of the way they really look, to the best of their skill level as artists.

Putting their collective knowledge about child development to work, the teachers explain wonderfully how art is a measure of development, a way to track growth over time. And, indeed, there is tremendous development in the tale of Lucas's two trees. The first is barely discernable as a tree, while the second rendition is more fully covered in color and detail—blue sky, yellow sun, green grass.

The tree, rather than a solid lump of trunk, now has branches top to bottom, and even branches growing from branches. The work appears more careful, less hasty.

And then I thought of this task while flipping through a heavy, giant collection of Mo Willems drawings and stories that I gave to Lucas as thanks for our time together. The anthology, entitled, *Don't Pigeonhole Me! Two Decades of the Mo Willems Sketchbook*, includes some art very unlike the style most often used in his published children's books. Willems uses stamps in his sketchbook rather often, and this piece of his work immediately caught my eye:

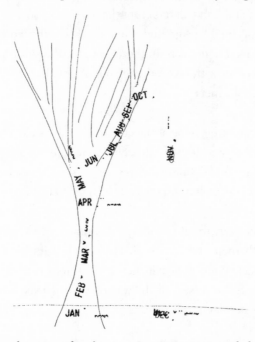

This, I thought, *is a tale of a tree.* In one image, with barely any drawing or text, it tells the story of how a tree regenerates year after year. It isn't especially true to life as an image in the literal sense, but it is true to the life cycle of a tree. Its simplicity is what makes it complex.

Through the lens of child development and in the context of school, children are pigeonholed. Depending on their abilities and dispositions, they are put in boxes: gifted, ADHD, smart, slow, ahead, behind, special ed, Asperger's. Performance is treated in evaluative "levels" so as to be quantifiable and measured. A more advanced child will have a more accurate, realistic drawing of a tree. We are trained to understand this as teachers, and we train children to understand this as learners. Mrs. Norbert and Mrs. Beverly correctly explain to families that as children remain under the influence of school for many years, they start to "represent the world they see with their eyes versus that which they imagine in their minds."

But the world I see with my eyes is not always a beautiful one. Sometimes my imagination frees me up to see a more beautiful world, and I wish I could draw that one. Having been in school for quite some time, I have learned to be realistic and accurate in my own representations. With every advanced degree comes further training in how to document and critique the world as it is rather than imagine it and create it as it could be. Lucas is at the beginning of his long journey through school, and despite his resistance he is learning to accept his training in order to become more "advanced."

Mo Willems offers an alternative. In his interview on the radio, I hear a possibility for Lucas that might free him up from a world of rules—a world in which success is equated with imitation rather than imagination:

> I hated drawing circles. I hated Mickey Mouse. I hated the stretch and squash, circley cute stuff. A circle inherently starts to look three-dimensional and that point, the Disney animators called it the "imitation of life." It's one of the reasons I

hated them because who the hell wants to imitate life? Here's a chance to make magic and you're going out and imitating life. That just seemed like a waste. I want to create joy, but a unique nonliving beauty.

Even if he never gets to drive that bus, I hope The Lucas always reserves his right to make magic, to make joy, to make his own unique world of nonliving beauty.

Part Two

The Crossroads School

IN A LANDSCAPE of ever-increasing school segregation nationwide, the Crossroads School is a multiethnic, multiracial, multilingual breath of fresh air. Located in an urban center and considered a "city school," it serves a community representing a lively collection of national heritages, and many children have recently arrived in the United States as first-generation immigrants. This diversity is a celebrated cornerstone of the school's identity. Visitors are greeted by a stunning mosaic of child-created tiles featuring self-portraits etched into the façade of the school building.

Students are mixed by social class, too, as the school is situated in a neighborhood that draws from households on all points along the economic spectrum. The daughters of upper-middle-class hipsters and elite university professors learn alongside the sons of mothers facing periodic homelessness despite working two jobs.

No exception to the larger demography of the teaching profession, the school faculty is composed largely of white women, with a handful of men, women of color, and several teachers and other staff members who identify as queer. The result of a principal with a keen, critical analysis of the relationship between schools and society, Crossroads has a strong commitment to families, to community, and to social justice. In big ways and small, the school reflects its central mission to nurture in students the desire and ability to meet the obligations of justice—to reject cruelty in their everyday interactions and to embrace their power as change makers and social actors.

As I am waiting to be buzzed in, I notice the sign "Keepin' it Green. We compost here." Coming up the stairwell, I am struck by a collection of decorative antidiscrimination tiles meant to make children aware of and sensitive to various sources of structural inequality: racism, ableism, sexism, ageism. A display of student work nearby features photos of children acting out emotions, prompting the viewer to "guess how we feel"—an effort to develop empathy and awareness of social and emotional cues. And in the hallway where there is a large bulletin board about being a leader, I am impressed by one of the identified characteristics: "Being a leader is being rebellious against unfair rules."

In its central mission statement, the school touts a belief that "the learner can be trusted" and "the teacher is also a learner." In an effort to mediate unequal power relationships between adults and children, students call their teachers by first name. No school uniforms are required, and teachers dress casually for work—jeans and sneakers are welcome and typical. There is tremendous pride among the faculty, who regularly post on a visible community bulletin board about the things they love, celebrate, and hope for in the collective space of their school building.

Emily Coogan was in her sixth year as a teacher at the Crossroads School when I met her. A young white woman born and raised in Iowa, Emily came to the northeast for college and ended up staying for the long haul. She is a no-frills kind of person. Her long brown hair was most often pulled back in a ponytail, she doesn't use makeup, and she wears jeans or corduroys with sweaters and long-sleeve Ts in basic, earthy tones. Our year together was her first teaching first grade, though she had worked with young children before.

In keeping with the tone of the overall school community, Emily believes in treating kids according to a high standard of academic rigor and social accountability. Her lessons are always carefully planned, particularly in the area of literacy. She is intentional and clear in her academic objectives, consistently drawing on rich children's literature and on the latest research in best practices in teaching and learning. Her materials are meticulously prepared and organized, and she regularly uses differentiated teaching practices: leveraging partner and small-group work, working one-on-one with struggling students, carefully grouping children in thoughtful ways, regularly assessing her learners. She relies on strategies that foster independence in young readers and writers: introducing self-monitoring and clarifying, tracking questions and curiosities with Post-it notes, using checklists and other available resources for independent editing.

Because Emily works so hard on her lessons, it can be particularly frustrating for her when noncompliant behavior interrupts her instructional flow. She tries various strategies here, too, to signal her authority in nonpunitive, nonauthoritative ways. "I'm wearing the hat right now," she says while donning a silly cap with a pinwheel on its top. "That means it's my turn to talk and your turn to listen. I'm teaching right now." A self-described "nonauthoritarian," she has a quiet, measured voice with children and is committed to a consistently steady, calm tone. Even when the kids test her patience—which they tirelessly do—she rarely raises her voice and is careful with her language and approach. She often tries to urge the children to do the right thing by encouraging them to "be flexible," to "persevere," and to take breaks and return when ready. She is often heard saying, "I believe in you."

Emily's classroom was spacious, and though it was never messy it somehow felt crowded—especially when children were seated on the rug for whole-class lessons and read-alouds. Kids were allowed to use chairs set up along the border, or even to stand up along the room's edges when necessary. Still, there was much elbowing and vying for space; the rug area was a hot spot for conflict.

Fostering independence in young learners is one of Emily's core commitments, and she often spoke of it as one of her most important values as an educator. "My goal is to set up systems where everything is accessible so they can work on their own," she explains. "I want them to be able to be independent; that's the biggest piece of my teaching." Her first concern about my presence was that the kids might see me as an adult on whom to lean for help, which she did not find desirable. "For me, it's always about teaching them how to be learners," she said, continuing, "Like, what it means to set goals and achieve them, what it means to be curious. Just knowing how to be a learner, how to be a member of a community; these are the two biggest things I want for them, especially in the younger grades. For some kids who don't see themselves as confident, I want to change that—to change that nonconfident identity so they can see themselves as agents of their own learning."

Similarly, in keeping with the value she places on independence and on teaching internal self-regulation, she does not consistently use a classroom management system of rewards and punishments, and her posted classroom rules are simple and streamlined:

1. Be Safe and Kind
2. Persevere (Keep Trying)
3. Listen
4. Solve Problems

Despite this, she did occasionally try behavior modification systems for individuals and for the whole class—sometimes giving and taking away tally marks or other kinds of points that resulted in earned or lost privileges. These were tested periodically but most often abandoned because keeping them up was tiring and unsustainable.

There is a small desk in the back of Emily's classroom, facing the wall, where children may be sent or may voluntarily choose to "take a break." Emily has posted a poem there that the children are to recite to themselves in order to help them independently manage their feelings and ready themselves once more for classroom engagement:

When angry feelings start to mount,
that's when I take some time to count.
Counting helps me settle down,
counting helps to fade my frown.

A school psychologist, too, often comes in to teach lessons about how to manage emotions and stay calm. On one occasion, she has the children sing a revised version of "If You're Happy and You Know It":

If you're angry and you know it, take a breath
If you're angry and you know it, take a breath
If you're angry and you know it, tell a friend to help you
    through it
If you're angry and you know it, take a breath

The educators are trying to provide strategies for calming down and self-regulating in these various ways, and Emily often tries to model them. "I'm feeling very frustrated today," she says one day when the children are particularly difficult to manage. "I am taking some deep breaths to try to calm down." But the children don't seem to take the suggestions seriously. Despite the emphasis on independently learning to solve problems, Emily regularly feels the need to intervene in resolving conflicts, and she is constantly putting out fires. "This year I just feel like I have so many kids who need to be held accountable," she tells me. "There are so many kids

I need to be on top of, so I couldn't be consistent. I couldn't keep up any systems. It just felt like there were too many kids needing to be held accountable all the time." In years past, she felt she was able to build a community of independent learners who held themselves, and one another, accountable. This year felt very different to her, and she expressed much sadness and disappointment. "I was exhausted at the end of every day," she tells me. "It was hard to enjoy. There were so many days when I didn't even want to come to school."

I often felt and shared Emily's frustration, saddened by the children's constant interruptions of her well-designed lessons. Though the two children profiled in the pages that follow did stand out in terms of the extremity of their behaviors, they were by no means the only ones who challenged the rules and routines. Several children poked and prodded, called out and acted silly at the wrong times, disengaged and caused mayhem. Emily tried many strategies and received much support from additional school staff, but the tone of the classroom remained exhausting from day to day. She was applying to graduate programs during our year together, hoping to leave the classroom for a short stint to pursue graduate studies.

Still, Emily proved able to call up bright moments—flashes of light and hope where children supported, encouraged, and respected both the teacher and one another. "I remember one day when things felt amazing," she begins to tell me. "A bunch of people were in here observing writing, and the kids were working on persuasive letters. And one boy says to another, 'Okay, let's be serious with this. Let me really pretend to be your dad and you read me your letter. I'll tell you if it's good enough to convince me.' And the other child responds, 'Well, if you're gonna be my dad, you need to be bald.' And the three of us laughed, but the best part was that then, after that, they had this real conversation as writers, really helping each other to improve their writing. It was just that kind of connection where they help each other as people and as learners that I so much want to see. It feels amazing when it's working well. Oh my gosh!"

Toward the end of the year, too, when the pressures of a fast-paced curriculum begin to ease up, Emily was able to find more joy in being with the children. The school days were generally intensive, for both her and the children. They had four straight hours of instruction without a break every morning, as a stroke of bad scheduling luck left her without specials or other prep times until late afternoon each day. The children did not have a regular recess time, and the lunch break was short. Even snack was sometimes accompanied by some kind of instruction. Children rarely had good opportunities to just mess around—to talk, to play, to enjoy free time.

But by the end of the year, when instructional demands finally started to quiet down, Emily took advantage of the possibility for some "family time" together. She smiles while telling me about the last day of school: "I really enjoyed our last day. We had such a nice morning, actually, and one of my favorite things about the end of the year is that I could relax, and I sort of made a decision with them—usually I'd pretty much teach to the end of the year, but we decided to give that up a bit. We weren't doing anything in particular, but everybody was engaged in something. I don't even remember what, exactly. I had four kids on my lap and we were all just goofing around, and it felt like—it just felt like I was interacting with them as humans instead of as students. I loved that."

The next chapters offer the chance to meet Sean and Marcus, two of Emily's first graders, as both students and human beings.

Sean

On Being Willful

It's a Sunday morning in mid-April and I have an appointment to be at Sean's house for a visit. I plan a Dunkin' Donuts stop en route and ask Sean's mother, Kate, if they would like anything. A chocolate frosted donut for Sean is requested. When the first store is out, I know better than to show up empty-handed or with some attempt at a substitute. Sean is not exactly a flexible kid—he is stubborn and insistent—so I know it's worth stopping at another location to secure his request.

I arrive at the house a bit early and am greeted by a black cat creeping around. It's an adorable house in a fairly urban neighborhood—yellow with white trim. It looks renovated compared to several of the surrounding houses. They have a neighbor closely adjoined on one side, and a driveway on the other—a rare and prized perk in these city parts. I notice a black BMW SUV with a child's bike in the trunk and wonder if the bike belongs to Sean.

Sean comes to the door quickly when I knock, clearly eager for my visit. He is in his typical T-shirt and sweatpants, which he dons regardless of the weather. His mom always sends him to school with extra layers, and those layers are always shed by the time morning circle starts. He prefers to travel light: no frills, no nonsense, no additional annoyances. He's a scrawny little guy with pale white skin and hair so blond that it, too, is almost white. There's just a hint of red to it, belying his Irish roots. He has small green eyes and a wide, mischievously bright smile.

"It's you," he says, with his slight and charming lisp. "You blink too fast."

This is his well-established greeting to me, having once made the observation in our time together at school that I blink too much, apparently. The comment is his way of connecting, establishing relationship. He has other disparaging observations, but this is his favorite. Luckily I have thick skin, developed over many years of young children telling me the unfiltered truth. I shake my head and roll my eyes in predictable response—also part of our routine— and step inside.

I am struck by the clean and modern design of the house, its high ceiling and sparse, careful decoration. There's an aluminum shoe tray and coat rack at the entrance, and Sean's little Air Jordans and canvas slip-ons are perfectly lined up and paired at the doorway. I add my Converse.

Just outside of their front door sits a beautiful white orchid plant, which I later learn was a gift from a previous neighbor. Sean and his mom lived elsewhere in this neighborhood up until about a year ago. They moved because this house is much bigger, but Sean is not entirely thrilled about it. Ilan, his favorite friend at school, moved to their old street just after they relocated to this new house—a big disappointment. Another classmate lives nearby, though, as does a friend from pre-K, who now attends a different school. Kate comments on how nice it is to have this community of folks and friends nearby, especially as she is raising Sean on her own. It's just the two of them. She left him with neighborhood friends when she was in New York for a business trip a couple of weeks back. "It's a big help to have that support nearby," she says. "And Sean really needs people around. I need to fill as much of his day as possible—we pack a lot in."

I soon learn that Sean is headed to his auntie and *tio*'s house for a sleepover, since he's on a school break starting the next day and his mom has to work. This extended family proves an important resource and another support for both Kate and Sean. He has three cousins there: five-year-old twins, a boy and a girl, and their seven-year-old sister. Kate says they're the "perfect age and gender mix" for Sean. I can tell he's excited about the visit. Kate has a big family—she's one of four—and all her siblings live relatively nearby. Her parents still live in her childhood home, just about an hour away. She seems close to her family and says that all of her brothers and sisters have children around Sean's age, which is wonderful for him, particularly since he's an only child. He has a sibling-like relationship with several of these cousins.

Kate strikes me as full New England material, suited well for those parts—a confident, intelligent, and professionally successful woman working in marketing. She wears glasses, a modern style that suits her face well, and has long blond hair in a style that clearly requires maintenance—a fact that is evident even on this casual Sunday morning. When I first arrive, she's sitting at the breakfast counter drinking her coffee and working on her laptop. The TV is on, set to *SpongeBob*, and Sean is walking around the living room, watching the show while simultaneously playing a game on his Samsung tablet.

A beautiful art set—markers, pastels, watercolors, paints—is sitting open on the living room floor, as is Sean's *SpongeBob* coloring book. I tell Kate that she shouldn't let me interrupt anything they would normally be doing today.

"This is it," she replies. "You're looking at it."

Willful Disputes

"Can we have a tickle fight?" Sean asks his mom.

"Maybe later."

"When you're done with your coffee?"

"We'll see."

"How about in five minutes?"

"Come have your donut."

The kitchen has beautiful marble countertops and new cabinets, and the breakfast counter has four small square stools with floral fabric. We all sit at the counter while Sean eats. It's where his mom's computer is set up and he seems to like being near her.

While Kate and I are talking, perhaps because he is feeling untended or overlooked, Sean begins banging both his fists on one of the stools, hard and with a lot of energy. Kate tells him to stop several times.

"It's too loud," she says.

"I like that," he responds. He continues drumming.

"Stop. It's bad for the furniture."

"I'm almost done." She allows him to continue. Or, at least, she gives up the fight. Eventually he stops on his own.

"I like the old house better. My room was bigger."

"That's true, but everything else in this house is bigger. You didn't have a playroom in the old house. And we didn't have a dining room."

"Yes, we did."

"No, we didn't. We had a kitchen."

"Yeah, we ate in the kitchen. That was our dinner room."

I'm quickly exhausted by the rapid volley of their conversation, the arguments. But Kate doesn't seem tired. She's patient and level and engaged. She treats her small son like a person worth negotiating with.

Their dining room seems to be a prized space for Kate, and it is gorgeous, with an elegant set of table and chairs. The living room, too, is beautiful and spacious, with a large leather chair facing the TV and a soft, worn couch to the right of the chair. Sean is climbing and jumping and doing headstands on the leather chair while talking to us. It's his way of being with us; he's there but his body is moving almost nonstop.

"I have a TV. I have a DS and a Wii and a game console and a tablet and a phone." He announces this proudly.

"You don't really have a phone," says mom.

"I do!"

"No, you don't." It turns out to be an old iPhone that he uses for gaming. "I do. And I'm going to bring it to the sleepover."

"No," says mom firmly, sounding definitive. But then she adds, "Why?"

"Because you bring yours! So that's not fair."

"People actually call me on my phone. I do work on my phone. Plus, I'm a grown-up. So I need a phone for real." While most parents start and end negotiations with, *I'm a grown-up, so that's why*, Kate offers more elaborate and thorough explanations and rationales. Grown-ups don't automatically have more rights or authority in Kate's view, and her treatment of Sean reflects this. Her initially firm "no" is followed by a more flexible and patient "why," so she can hear out his reasoning. He's given some authority and power in decision making, some freedom and choice at home. When Kate does give a firm directive, Sean often ignores it initially, and this is not something Kate takes as a personal affront or a sign of disrespect. She takes it as the starting point for negotiations, a time to explain her thinking and hear out his.

His mom asks him to go upstairs and get all the stuff he wants to take to his cousins' house. He brings down the old iPhone and a very worn, reddish little stuffed alien toy. "It's very dirty but I need it. I got it when I was four. I need it to sleep."

"Are you *really* going to bring that?" mom asks, with a momentary tone of negative judgment.

"*Yes*," Sean replies with a strong edge. "I *am*."

"Okay," says Kate, shaking her head ever so slightly.

"Chocolate milk," says Sean, intending a request. He's aggressive in his approach, and Kate reminds him, with a level voice but several times, that she is waiting for a full sentence. She refuses chocolate milk but agrees to strawberry.

"You have to drink it at the breakfast counter," she says. "Not in the living room." He comes over, takes one quick sip, and then leaves it behind to tend to the multiple distractions in the living room. Kate redirects him to finish it and he does, but hardly in one fell swoop. He dawdles and spins from spot to spot, his attention not sustained.

Our attention turns to a TV show Sean has recorded—a show called *How It's Made* on the Science Channel. He has already seen this episode, and I'm watching with interest, as they are explaining how accordions are made. At first I can't tell what they are putting together, so I look puzzled. Sean is playing on his tablet but looks up briefly to inform me that they're making accordions. I am clearly interested and I read some of the subtitles to him since the people featured are speaking Italian. We enjoy the show together.

In the next segment we're learning how wasabi is made. I don't know how many times Sean has seen this episode, but he for sure knows how to make wasabi. As we begin to hear about the process, his mom gets interested and comes away from her computer at the breakfast counter. "Scootch over," she says to Sean on the couch, moving him to the side.

He playfully refuses, "I'll *never* move!" so they tickle and tumble a bit. When they finish tussling and she has secured a spot for herself against the arm of the couch, Sean puts his tablet away and moves his body to her side for some snuggling. She holds him close. A few moments later he moves even closer to her, and it's obviously a familiar and affectionate position for both. In my time with him at school he never struck me as particularly cuddly or even sweet. He's a feisty little rascal with a strong, willful edge and an assertive, questioning personality. At this moment, though, he is a loving mother's baby.

He seems content, with everyone's full attention and together-ness on the couch, and he quiets down and settles in with a calm body. He is perfectly still and intently focused—a rare event. We are all watching with interest the wasabi-making process. He is excited to be expert, as compared to us two adults. "The wasabi comes from a plant," he explains, before the show can get to that part. "They need hot springs water at a specific temperature for it and it has to be really clean water. They use flamethrowers."

Here his mom interrupts: "Flamethrowers? For what? What are you talking about?" She challenges his authority on the subject for a moment.

"For the roots. You'll see. The spicy stuff is in the roots of the plant. They use sharks' teeth to grate it."

Most of these facts turn out to be accurate as the details un-fold. His mom does clarify that it is sharks' skin, not teeth, used to grate the wasabi root in the upscale Japanese restaurant featured. I can't help but be impressed by him. He obviously not only lis-tened carefully, but also understood the entire process of making wasabi through many rapid subtitles and some large vocabulary. He uses clear, confident language in his explanation as he teaches us. He is focused, engaged, and expert. This is not the Sean I see at school—often seemingly distracted, disengaged, disruptive.

During a commercial his mom and I begin to talk, which he does *not* like. He puts his hand over her mouth while she is in the middle of speaking. I worry about a harsh and uncomfortable repri-mand, considering for a brief moment what my own mother would have done to me in such a situation—but to my surprise Kate rea-sons with him. "It's okay for us to talk during a commercial. What is so compelling about this commercial?" From her language, I see how he so easily comprehended the large vocabulary in the television show.

"There's a funny part."

"All right. After this show, we're done with TV." It's not a punishment, just a statement.

"What are we gonna do then?"

"We'll have to think of something."

"Like what? Wii?"

"We'll see."

"The park?"

"We will see."

Now that his mind is fixed on the park, he's done with the show even though I had been eager to see it through to its end. He doesn't stop to consider what the rest of us might want; he's up off the couch, ready to rumble, and tells his mom he wants to take his scooter.

They argue about what shoes to wear. He wants Crocs; she wants sneakers; they settle on canvas slip-ons.

They argue about what coat to wear. She wants a big and warm one; he wants a flimsy sweatshirt. They settle on a fleece he usually wears for skiing.

They argue about his helmet. She wants him to wear it; he doesn't. He gives up that fight and they get it out of the car.

They argue about whether the scooter needs WD-40. He insists it does and tries to command her to get it. She says he should ride and then she'll decide whether it's necessary.

Dispute after dispute—willful negotiations, willful arguments, willful challenges to the authority of his mother. I am tired. But, again, and amazingly, Kate is not. She genuinely doesn't believe in authority for its own sake. She believes in giving Sean space, treating him as though his opinions and his desires matter. "He can be challenging in that he is just a questioner about everything," Kate tells me when asked to describe him. "He won't let anything go. Everything needs to be explained; he needs to be part of the process. If he's not happy with your answer, he doesn't let it go." She laughs.

I think about his teacher at this moment, though, and how *unfunny* she finds this trait. I can't think of many teachers who would find constant, persistent, tireless questioning easy to manage in the context of a full classroom of children—all with different questions and desires, needs and demands. "Does he get that trait from you?" I ask.

"No, I'm not at all like that. So it's very interesting for me to see that. I have much more of a pleasing aspect to me; I'll try and compromise and collaborate, but he will not. He is very much like, *No, no, no, why, I don't want to do this, I don't want to do that, how about if I do this other thing.* He can wear on you with all that!" She laughs again. "He's just a questioner. If you tell him he has to do something just because it's what you do at school, that won't work. He wants to know *why* you have to do it at school, and sometimes, really, there just isn't a good reason. For me, at home, if he jumps up at the dinner table, I would rather he sit and eat his supper, but it's not really the end of the world if he doesn't. For the things we do here at home, it just doesn't matter."

At home, with just one child and plenty of room for free choice, dispute and negotiation are options—ones that Kate allows because she believes questioning is a positive and valuable habit. "It doesn't help him at school, I know," she says, "but I think it will help him in life."

Willful Demands

Kate tells Sean that he gets to scoot around one lap of the raceway at the park, and then it will be time to head home for lunch. Predictably, a dispute ensues.

"I already had lunch!"

"That was breakfast."

"Three laps."

"One lap."

The dispute is interrupted when Sean becomes distracted by a group of teenagers playing flag football. He looks at them with an envious gaze. He starts his one lap, falls down trying a fancy trick, and with the start of tears says, "Mom, I kind of hurted myself!" I'm ashamed to wonder if he's really hurt or merely trying to engage her sympathy so as to earn a second lap.

"Oh yeah, you're right. You did. But no blood." He gets up and back on his scooter.

McDonald's is across the street, and this now catches his attention. He puts on his most belligerent and aggressive tone and announces clearly, twice: "I want a hamburger." It's as if he knows this demand will be a full-on fight and tries to head it off with a particularly insistent approach.

"No." Matching his insistence, she uses a strong and stern tone.

"I want a hamburger," he repeats.

"Not today."

"I want a hamburger"—broken-record-style.

"You're not gonna have one." Kate replies with a comeback to each and every of his repeated pleas for a hamburger. Eventually, for the first time seeming tired, she says, "Well, I want a quiet kid. We can't all get what we want."

Exasperated now, he loudly exclaims, *"Well, I'm going to get a hamburger!"* And he rolls away from us on his scooter in the direction of McDonald's.

"Okay, bye," she says, and we begin walking away. She is calm and doesn't look back. "He's usually pretty good about coming back," she tells me. And though he's losing the hamburger fight, I realize that he has covertly earned himself a second lap around the park.

Completing it, and returning to us, he declares, "Okay, I had my hamburger!" Pretending and performing his feigned victory keeps his pride intact. Plus, his mood is good on account of that extra lap. "Push me on the tire swing?" he asks sweetly. He is on to the next order of business and this time is going for a more polite and charming approach. She agrees, despite lunch hour having arrived. Upon his request, too, she races him to the swing.

He pushes his shoes off while swinging, and Kate is annoyed. A negotiation ensues that ends in a compromise: he can go shoeless on the swing, but when it's time to get off, no nonsense about putting them back on.

"After this I want to go on the spinning dish," he announces.

"I'll be too tired to spin you." I wonder if she's forgotten about lunch, which could serve as another good reason to deny his request.

Looking in my direction now, he says, "Well, she can." And he points to me with a sly and full smile that is characteristically Sean. As if I exist for his benefit. I'm torn. The teacher in me wants to say no—just for the sake of it, because he's been told it's time to go, we are way past that announcement, and I didn't offer to spin anyone on anything. At this moment, though, trying to take an empathic stance and mirror the way Kate chooses to parent him, I decide to see how it feels to agree.

I was trained in consistency, in following through when you say something is going to happen, in insisting on authority and on having the final word. In the end, though, he got to spin. And then we went home and there was still time for lunch. And he was headed to his auntie and *tio*'s right on time. Was all well that ended well?

Meeting the majority of Sean's demands at home did not seem terribly problematic, but juxtaposing that response with what happens at school raises a number of questions. When Sean makes willful demands of his teacher and his peers, they do not and cannot match Kate's generous responsiveness.

One morning, the class is playing a game during community circle. A child closes her or his eyes while another child says a phrase in a disguised voice, hoping not to be correctly identified. Justin, a kind of nerdy and ever-cooperative child, gets to go first because Emily says he has really been "a leader" this week. He is being rewarded for his good behavior. Sean is displeased by the choice. Justin is often his foil in the classroom, and they have many conflicts. Not to mention, unsurprisingly, Sean had wanted to be the one to go first.

Sean knows enough to understand that school is not home, and he can't use the "I want a hamburger" approach to make a demand at school. It is much too direct and obvious, and he has enough training in the culture of school to know it will not do. So he has developed much more complex and covert ways of making demands. Thus, when he wants to demand that *he* go first and that *he* be identified as a "leader" for once, he becomes uncooperative.

"Justin, you are standing *way* too close to me!" Sean announces with an aggressive style, and he pushes Justin further away.

"Sean, use your words, not your body," says Emily sternly. "Go ahead and guess, Justin."

"Is it Laura?" Justin guesses, correctly.

"You are such a cheater, Justin! You always cheat," says Sean.

"Sean, that is not okay. You need to play well with us or else take a break." The whole point of the game is to build community, to start the day with some fun as a group. Sean is undercutting that goal with his behavior and is threatened with ejection from the community Emily is trying so hard to cultivate.

Sean wants to have a turn, but his behavior is preventing Emily from being able to choose him. "Laura, go ahead and take a turn," says Emily. Sean stews.

"Is it Myla?"

She is supposed to get two guesses, but Sean calls out, "*No!* Wrong. It was Aravind."

"I could have had two turns!" Laura is not pleased. In the next round, Sean does the very same thing, announcing the person before the child has had a second guess. Presumably he is trying to move the game along before time runs out so that he will get a turn; I see him looking at the clock quite often. He bosses people around by telling them to sit still or take a guess, trying to lead and take control of the group. He criticizes children who guess incorrectly with insults and unsolicited advice about how they might do better next time. He is loud, upsetting to other children, who often respond by meeting him with an insulting retort, and it results in Emily having to end the game early. Where Sean had tried the entire time to demand a turn, his behavior ends up preventing his hopes of having a turn—and, to boot, he ruins the game for the other children and disrupts Emily's attempt to build community. Though he is not yet punished by exclusion from the group, the other children are upset with him—so in this sense he has been excluded.

"Let's close the game," Emily announces. "It's clear we can't play anymore." Sean now turns his behavior up a notch, demanding a turn more directly and saying it's "not fair" for everyone not to get a turn. "Enough," says Emily with her calm tone. "I'm going to check in with you in a minute, Sean."

"You're a burp girl," he says to Maria, the child with misfortune enough to be standing next to him—in the wrong place at the wrong time.

"What? You are mean. You better check yourself!" she responds, putting her face close to his. This is not a classroom of children who roll over easily. They are spirited and spunky, and most of them do not accept mistreatment lightly.

"Take a break, Maria," Emily says sternly. Maria is often in trouble so is not treated as a victim in this instance. Maria is now obviously frustrated, looking at Sean with disgust. "Sean, you take a break, too," says Emily as an afterthought. Maria looks only mildly appeased. And Sean doesn't seem to mind taking a break. Reading comes next and he's not eager to move forward in the nongame parts of the school day.

But then Emily reminds the other children that it's time to line up for art, and Sean seems to realize he made a tactical error. His face turns bright red. He sits down in the take-a-break spot at the back of the room for a full ten seconds or so, and then he rushes over to Emily to hastily try to make amends.

"What are you thinking about when you're taking a break?" she asks, part of the routine to get out of the time-out.

"Getting ready," he replies obediently.

"You're thinking about being ready. Maybe you think about taking deep breaths. Maybe you think about how you will return with a calm body." Sean looks at the clock, giving away his preoccupation with art. "You're not ready," Emily decides, and she takes the other children and leaves him behind. When she returns, the conversation starts back up.

"On a break, you are thinking about being ready," she says.

"Okay."

"You are trying to calm yourself down," she continues.

"Okay, okay, okay. Can I go to art now?" He is obviously upset, but when finally released to art he walks backward and spins around with every step—maybe to save face, maybe again as a display of pride and a way to ward off embarrassment, especially with me there as witness.

Sean makes several demands of his classmates in my time with him at school, and they are rarely kindly worded. They are generally abrupt and sharp: *Stop talking! Leave me alone. Get away from me! You be my partner.* With Justin in particular, he often makes demands that undercut the view of Justin as perfect. When Justin gives a very thorough, astute, and warmly rewarded response to an instructional question, Sean looks displeased. "You know what, Justin?" he begins. "You really should monitor your airtime."

Emily is once again let down by the kind of communication happening between kids in her room. Unlike Kate, she is tired. Exhausted, really. "I just couldn't make the classroom community what I wanted it to be," she tells me at the end of the year. "I couldn't build the community that I typically feel like I can put in place." Emily tried many strategies for addressing behavior—a combination of interventions for individual children and more communal accommodations. Near the end of the year, for example, she tried to engage the children in understanding the particular needs of individual children. "Sean needs space," she tells the kids one day while they are crowded together on the rug. "I notice that some kids need a lot of space and others need only a little. Make sure you have a little bubble of space around you with your arms, and give Sean a little extra."

The kids shuffle around a bit, adjusting to try to each win some small territory. "Sean, do you have enough space? This is your chance. Give yourself enough space." Sean seems to appreciate the special attention and treatment, but on other occasions on the rug this becomes a demand he himself makes.

"Guys, can you please give me some space?!" His demand lacks Emily's mature and level delivery, and the other children are wary. Still, they move over a bit to give him extra room, remembering that Emily asked them to be considerate on this point. They have to squeeze together tightly. With his newfound space, Sean decides to lie down. The girl next to him doesn't like this, so she makes a production of moving closer to him to win back some of her original space. He becomes furious. "Oh my god!" he exclaims. "Can you get away from me and stay away from me?" Now he's fully ramped up, rolling around, folding his body over, laying himself down in a way that requires an unreasonable amount of space. Emily has been unable to start the math lesson due to all the commotion. Nearly fifteen minutes is spent this way.

"Sit *up*," she says, more sharply than usual. He remains lying down but puts his legs in the air in an effort at weak compromise. This might have worked at home, but it does not work with Emily. This time she has made the demand, and she is insistent. *"All the way,"* she instructs. He sits up until the lesson begins and then returns to lying down. He is sent to take a break, and he misses the lesson.

Several of Sean's demands result in the loss of privileges for the other children. Games end early. Kids lose some of their space to afford him extra. And once, making a demand for some of a classmate's snack resulted in the new rule that nobody was allowed to share food anymore. The nature of his willful demands not only got him in trouble quite often, but also left him on the outskirts of social life and excluded him from the small bit of community that managed to form among the children.

Willful Disruptions

Often left out socially, Sean apparently subscribed to a philosophy of *If you can't join them, beat them.* Or, put another way, if he wasn't going to be included in the classroom in the particular ways that he wanted, then he was going to willfully disrupt those activities. In much the same way that he disrupted the morning circle game, he also disrupted many academic lessons.

"Gather up," Emily announces, as it is time for a read-aloud. The children begin to gather on the rug, and Sean wants to see the front of the book before she has revealed the title. "What's the book?" he asks. Emily ignores him, as he is already out of line. His job is to settle in and wait to find out. Still, he has made a demand to know and expects it to be met, and he now realizes the full class is gathered as witness. He is at the front—the staging area. "Oooh, I want to kiss it," he says, pretending to smooch the book. He looks back at his classmates for a laugh or other affirmation and is smiling to himself, pleased with his own humor. Emily, however, is displeased and he quickly becomes angry or, perhaps, embarrassed. Neither Emily nor the other children found his joke funny. "I'm taking a break!" he announces, and he moves to the back of the room, once again missing a lesson.

Emily begins to read, but Sean does not seem done with his disruption. He walks over to Emily's desk and begins playing with her teacher markers. "Yes, a fat one!" He begins waving it around like a sword, again looking to his classmates for someone to notice him in humored appreciation. Nothing. He starts flipping through one of Emily's notebooks, gets bored, and meanders back over toward the rug. The kids are enjoying the book, reading the repetitious refrains together in chorus. Sean has not been included, so he disrupts; the next time they call out in unison, he says, "Great! It's nice and loud. *Let's party!*" Miraculously, both Emily and the other children manage to ignore him. His attempt to make himself noticed—visible—backfires. Now he is invisible. His attempt to be included renders him further excluded.

He kicks up the disruption, walking through the group of children gathered on the rug and standing directly in front of the book, blocking their view. Of course, this can't be ignored. He is bold and his disruption is brazen. Emily is impressively calm, sending him once more to take a break.

Though his disruptions are ill conceived and position him further outside the community, usually resulting in his full exclusion, he continues to try to use them as a way to feel included, to be connected, and to have fun. Even in my time with him at home, he used disruptive tactics to engage with me socially. Though he already had my undivided attention, he seemed to be entertained by disruption.

We are in the living room when he pulls out *Bop It!*—a handheld electronic game that has five possible actions. The toy barks out instructions indicating which actions the player should take, in rapid succession. "Spin it!" for example, and the player's job is to spin a particular end of the toy quickly enough to not be counted out for slowness. Part of the game's appeal, in addition to its fast and fun pace, is that it mocks you when you fail: "Focus! Concentrate!" it reprimands the player, and Sean finds it hilarious. At the start of the game, the toy announces the current high score—29—but Sean insists his high score is actually 40. This, of course, is not possible. Still, he is good at it. He takes a turn and gets a very impressive 22.

This is quite difficult to do. I try several times with little success, mostly because Sean gave me poor instructions. But now he's finding it enjoyable to see how badly I'm doing and when I tell him I am sure I can beat his high score, he ends up deciding to sabotage all my turns. He talks loudly so I won't hear the toy's instructions. He pulls on the wrong parts when it's my turn and when the toy is in my hands. He's having the absolute time of his life disrupting all my turns—far more fun than he has when it's his own turn to play. He refuses to pass me the toy when it is my turn. And even though I still want to try to compete with his high score, he puts the game away when he's bored with it, again showing no interest in my preferences.

Despite the way he behaves, Sean's mom describes him consistently as a "very social kid." It is undoubtedly true that he wants to be in relationship. Many of his antics are about clowning, trying to get a laugh from other kids, trying to be noticed by them. He spends an exorbitant amount of time at school trying to get the attention of one particular peer whom he considers his friend. Indeed, countless incidents of getting in trouble stem from his desire to inappropriately entertain and win the affection of this particular child.

Ilan, the central object of Sean's friendly affection, is himself a disruptive force in the classroom—loud and distractible, bursting with energy, active, physical, extroverted. Ilan is included, though, in the central group of boys who play together and work together at school. He is liked and accepted, though it seems he gets in trouble every bit as much as Sean. While he certainly gives Emily a run for her money, he is slightly less problematic and requires less of her attention overall because he gets his work done, doesn't aggravate his classmates as often through his disruptions, and is not as quick to become angry or have an outburst.

I often witness Sean vying for Ilan's attention and approval, overtly and covertly. Ilan is a central figure as I observe, interact with, and try to understand Sean. Sometimes Sean is trying to be with Ilan, trying to be near him, earnestly trying to get his attention.

One day Emily releases the kids to work with partners of their own choosing. Sean immediately beelines over to Ilan, who sees him coming and starts to scoot his body in the direction of another boy instead. Sean still pursues him. Ilan says, "I have a partner already," so Sean gets red, goes over to another pair of boys, and listens to their exchange while starting to fling a girl's sweatshirt that has been placed near him. Ilan is called over to read in a small group with Emily. Sean grabs his book and joins them despite not being directed to do so. As soon as the read-aloud begins—at the exact moment Emily starts—Sean gets up. He wanders toward the back of the room, wanders back, stands up in the circle, moves around, bumps Ilan, smiles at him devilishly, then sits back down next to him.

Other times they engage in disruption together, which is apparently fun for them both, as for example, when Sean engaged Ilan in playing swords with their pencils. Sean says, "Sean is a sissy," and in playful call-and-response, Ilan laughs and says, "Ilan is a butthead." This goes on for some time and both seem wildly amused. Then Emily threatens the loss of recess.

On still other occasions, Sean seems to pick a fight with Ilan on purpose, as if having his negative attention is better than having no attention at all. Sean is supposed to be working with his assigned partner, in his assigned partner spot. He instead decides to sit *on* Ilan, insisting that this is his spot. A huge argument ensues. "This is my partner spot," says Ilan. "See, my folder and writing are here!" Sean insists that Emily didn't say they had to use assigned partner spots. This is allowed to go on for some time, while Emily tries to gather her composure and figure out what to do. She comes over, lets it go on for a few moments while listening to them, and then says, "Okay. I'm going to ask both of you to stop." They do. "Thank you for stopping." She goes on to focus on Sean's choice to sit on Ilan instead of in an empty chair right next to Ilan. "There's a hard way and an easy way, Sean. The hard way is to sit on Ilan's body. The easy way is to be flexible and sit in the empty chair right here." Sean doesn't like it. He insists that Ilan is in an inappropriate spot. Eventually, Sean just walks away from Emily and Ilan both. Exhausted, Emily allows this. Eventually Sean returns to the empty chair next to Ilan.

In and through this kind of behavior, Sean is vying for Ilan's affection and attention. On one occasion, the children were working on a persuasive writing assignment that required them to make a request and to back it up with three reasons why that request should be met.

Ilan decides to persuade his mother to schedule a playdate with Sanjay, and this is upsetting to Sean. A long conversation and argument ensue about why Ilan won't request a playdate with Sean instead. Sean complains that Ilan almost never has playdates with him, and there is discussion and debate about this. Ilan names several examples of times they did have playdates. Neither child is using an aggressive tone; it is an honest and earnest conversation in which Sean is trying to understand and Ilan is trying to be somewhat sensitive. But Ilan insists he first wants the playdate with Sanjay, "and then with you, Sean." This seems to quiet Sean for a moment, but he still can't settle into his work. Ilan leaves his chair to sharpen a pencil, and Sean takes the chair.

I wonder if Sean is trying to use disruption as a way to reengage Ilan—as if fighting with him would still be a worthwhile interaction. But Ilan doesn't seem to mind that his chair is gone, which is surprising. Sean tries another disruption, accusing Ilan of copying his work. Now Ilan is becoming frustrated. Sean complains, clearly and in a way that makes me feel sad for him, "Ilan, you are way nicer to Sanjay than me." Ilan turns off his frustration and just shrugs his shoulders.

Sean is seeking social connection and tries many strategies—helpful and unhelpful, appropriate and inappropriate, honest and provocative—to secure it. Disruption plays an important part in his attempts to make friends. He is willing to play disruptive games and get in trouble if it means a good time. He is willing to leverage a classroom disruption to get a peer's positive affirmation. And he is willing to use disruption to get a peer's negative attention—seeming to prefer it to no attention at all. Importantly, too, sometimes the disruption is a way to cope with hurt feelings.

Both Emily and Kate describe Sean as deeply social, seeking connection. Still, being "social" doesn't just mean wanting to be around people; it also includes knowing how to be with those other people in a reciprocal relationship. Here Sean's social skills fall short and he too heavily relies on disruption, which most often then results in his exclusion from the community altogether.

Perhaps because he feels a general sense of nonbelonging and loneliness, Sean perceives unfairness in his relations with others and strongly reacts to any sense of slight. He often accuses other children of being disrespectful and yells at them in an accusatory tone—for looking at him the wrong way, for copying him, for stealing from him, for making fun of him, for crowding him, for bossing him. This makes other children avoid him.

Upon the instances of this kind of exclusion, Sean feels hurt and slighted rather than being able to understand how his own

behavior factors into his peers' response and his resulting loneliness. A feedback loop develops: a willing peer plays with him but
then becomes frustrated, so the peer leaves him and then Sean
becomes frustrated. He blames the peer and the peer blames him.
Emily describes it this way: "He's so sensitive, and he perceives
a slight, and then he gets angry, and then, like—then he starts
shouting at people. And if somebody even says, *Sean, could you
pass me my jacket*, he [responds] like, *Oh my god, you hit me!*
Right? That's what his response is, and then they have a hard time.
Then they get mad and he perceives that they're the person who
did something wrong to him, and so it just sort of creates this
negative environment."

His mother agrees that Sean experiences hurt feelings that then
result in the mistreatment of peers: "I know he has a problem
speaking quietly to other kids. He always had a problem with that.
He will speak in an unfriendly way and he won't—someone does
something to him and his feelings are so hurt, he can't make a
connection yet with empathy. Like, *What I want to get from other
people I should be putting out*. He can't get that yet." But his mother
adds, "He's just very, very social. He's very loving. He loves his
family. He loves his friends. He's just—he gets very emotionally
invested in people."

This additional perspective, this different angle, helps me to
see Sean as overly sensitive because he is loving, invested with
his whole heart, feeling deeply. It helps me to empathize with his
hurt feelings, which sometimes seem overblown to me and likely
to Emily, an overreaction to unintentional slights. The tone and
style he uses with other children rarely look, sound, or feel loving;
his mother reminds me that, ironically, his harsh approach stems
from how desperately he wishes to love and be loved by his peers.
His harshness is a misguided search for kindness, his disruptions a
misguided attempt at connection.

Willful Distractions

Sean tells me he likes to draw. "I use *all* this stuff," his says, pointing to the wide array of pastels, watercolors, crayons, and markers in his art set. But when I look through his *SpongeBob* coloring book I notice that he only uses crayon, and he does not have a single page complete. There's a little color on one page, a dab on the next, something small going on, on the third. He doesn't go in order page by page and he doesn't necessarily use the "right" colors for things. On one page he began coloring a giant hamburger bun with multicolored stripes. On another a snail is polka-dotted. Even if he's doing something he enjoys, he seems to like multitasking and he flits fickly from one activity to the next. At school, this is a problem.

Even his mother wishes for him to be slightly different—to be a kid who can play with Lego blocks or do puzzles, or read and color on his own. "He's just not that kid," she says. "He gets bored with things very easily." She felt much of this had to do with his needs and his nature as a boy—an idea she returned to often in our conversations. She referred to his distractibility multiple times as "boyish energy" and explained that she felt he needed time to run around, to be outdoors, to release that energy. She lamented how constraining schools were, how short his recess break was, how little he was able to move and yell and jump and run around.

Kate also felt he would benefit from a male role model at school and was disappointed when he wasn't assigned to the section of first grade that had a male teacher. "I think he feels the void," she says of Sean's feelings around not having his father present. In her view, some of his problems stem from the absence of a model who might show him ways to channel his boyish energy. She felt the school perceived his "home life to be a positive one," relative to many of the other children's situations, and therefore didn't consider the needs he might have as the son of a single mother. I wondered how the school's perception in this regard might be impacted by Sean's solid middle-class whiteness.

Despite these theories, which centered not just on Sean himself but on a more contextual view of his interactions with school and home life, Kate ultimately pursued a medical evaluation for Sean. Toward the end of the academic year, she reluctantly decided to talk to her pediatrician about the possibility of an ADHD diagnosis. Her sister, now an educator, had extraordinary difficulty paying attention when she was a young child in school. She played a part in convincing Kate that evaluating him was the right thing to do, telling her that she "wished someone had paid attention to me, had told me that maybe I wasn't dumb but just needed some help focusing." Kate was moved by her sister's experience, and she explains her decision and her reluctance: "I had him evaluated mostly because he had started fighting with his friends, and I had been concerned anyway because Emily was saying he's not where he should be academically and all this stuff. I wasn't too worried about that part because I know he's a bright kid, but then he started physically fighting and he was so unhappy about it, so I just thought maybe there's something that he needs help with. I took him to the pediatrician—she has known him since he was a baby and I trust her. She recommended that he be evaluated. She observed him, and I filled out the questionnaire, and I felt like I was reading a description of him. I mean, I really did . . ."

She takes a long pause, tears gathering. "It almost made me cry. Like, maybe I should have been more alert to this. The doctor is not one to jump to things and that's one thing that I've always liked about her, and she just felt like knowing him as long as she had, and doing some observations, reading the questionnaires—mine and Emily's were very consistent. She thought medication [for ADHD] was worth a try—that he really seemed like a classic kid who might just need a little help focusing. So we did start the medication and

I was very trepidatious about it. I was afraid it would change his personality. That was my biggest concern. I didn't want him to become a robot kid."

As it turned out, the medicine did not result in making him a "robot kid," but it did seem to make him extremely emotional. Though his academic work steadily improved—his handwriting much clearer, his written ideas much more focused, his assignments more frequently completed—in the final weeks of school, he cried almost daily. He didn't want to go to recess. He didn't want to participate in field day. He wanted his mom and often begged to go home to her. It was as if all the sensitivity and feeling hiding behind the mask of his disruptive behavior got unleashed, released, made visible.

There were many changes coming with the end of the year. Summer vacation would mean a good deal more loneliness. Emily was leaving for graduate school and he would have a new teacher in the coming year. Ilan announced a move to Texas, which was heartbreaking for Sean. All of this was fodder for tears. Still, both Kate and Emily felt the medication was contributing to his sadness. No longer able to distract his mind by flitting from one thing to the next, no longer able to use disruptions to dodge negative emotions and experiences, he seemed to *feel* more strongly and to have to face those feelings.

"He wasn't making you angry anymore?" I ask Emily.

"No. He was just making me sad. He kept saying, 'Nobody cares about me.'"

The medication seemed to allow Sean to express his feelings in ways that more accurately reflected them. When he felt sadness, he cried. Before the medication, when he felt sadness, he got angry and belligerent. It was hard to see sadness in those behaviors, which were exhausting and disruptive and therefore prevented others from feeling compassion toward him. He was no longer able to distract himself from the sadness, and revealing that sadness allowed his caregivers to resist getting distracted by his outbursts, instead starting to see them as reflections of hurt.

I have no doubt that Sean is naturally inclined to distractions. But I did often wonder if some of his distractibility was willful—an intentional effort to avoid tasks and emotions that he found unpleasant or unmanageable. Being impossible during solitary activities at home won him the attention of his mom, as well as her ongoing efforts to make sure that he had many playdates that helped him to avoid a sense of loneliness and boredom. Losing focus during a lesson allowed him (or forced him) to take a break—to escape—either to the classroom next door or to the noninstructional area of the room, to the hallway or the psychologist, to the principal's office or the bathroom. On many occasions during instructional time I found him sitting with the male janitor on the ground level of the building, chatting and laughing.

Sean was easily able to recenter and focus himself on the occasions when failure to complete his work had a consequence that meant something to him. "Emily, what happens if I don't finish this letter in time?" he asked one day. Time was running short, and he seemed to be making a calculated decision about whether or not to persist in the effort. When he learned that a short recess break would be next and that he would have to stay in to complete the work, I noticed that he got right down to business. "Guys," he said angrily to a rowdy group of kids near him, "can you please stop?! That clock says I only have two minutes left and I need to finish before recess!" He actively requested that they not distract him, settled in to work, and finished in time.

I became further convinced of some element of willful distraction when Sean and I spent time together, just a few days before the end of the school year. He was playing on my iPad while we chatted—adeptly managing our conversation and a game at the same time. I asked him about his sadness toward the end of the year.

"Well," he began, "Ilan and Susanna were making, like, a secret club and saying stuff about me. My mom already knows about it and if we talk about it more, it's gonna make me sad, so . . ." I listen and don't respond, keeping my eyes focused on the game. Both of us allow the game to be a distraction, a space of safety and comfort. "I like to talk about video games!" he continues, shifting his mood considerably, and he laughs. "That's what I do when I'm sad. Sometimes when sad stuff happens, I just like to play video games. That's so I don't have to talk about stuff or think about stuff when talking about it is making me sad." We let the music of the game fill the silence. But his mind is not fully distracted, and he returns to talking about the incident: "But it happened a long time ago, so, that's pretty good." Video games allow for intentional distraction, a place of escape from sad feelings.

In my view, "attention deficit" as willful distraction has a place in Sean's story. If feelings are painful, activities boring, tasks too demanding, allowing oneself to be distracted from them may be a strategy worth trying. Educators are not medical doctors; they cannot diagnose or treat ADHD in individual children. But context matters to a child's ability and willingness to stay focused, and this makes educators powerful actors. The culture of the classroom, its connectedness and community, can maximize or minimize a child's willful distraction. Still, Sean remained on medication prescribed to hold his focus and calm his mind.

Coda: Willful Defiance

Sean's willfulness—his willful disputes, demands, disruptions, and distractions—drew my attention in part because I had been closely following the story of a school board decision in California. In May of 2013, the Los Angeles Unified School District school board voted to end the practice of suspending and expelling students for "willful defiance"—a vague, subjective, and all-encompassing charge that included acts like mouthing off to a teacher, having a "bad attitude," refusing to take off a hat, and causing any classroom disruption.

The willful defiance charge accounts for 54 percent of suspensions and 25 percent of expulsions across the state of California. Many community groups, legislators, and educators argued against the use of willful defiance on the grounds that it violates young people's civil rights. Particularly because of the profoundly racialized application of the charge, with children of color egregiously overrepresented in the accusations of willful defiance, I am easily persuaded that its use is a civil rights violation.

But punishment for willful defiance does not only violate the individual civil rights of young people. It also threatens democracy more broadly. Sean's story illustrates this. He is actively, willfully defiant. Unlike children who may still be learning the culture of schooling—the expectations, the rules, the rewards and consequences—Sean is well aware of the culture. Indeed, when asked to draw what a "good attitude" looks like in school, he produced an image of Emily, labeled with her name, instructing him to "do it" through a speech bubble hovering overhead. Next to Emily, he drew himself and labeled his name, answering back, "OK. I'll try."

In Sean's view of school, the teacher's role is to issue a directive—"Do it"—and a child with a good attitude will compliantly agree to "try" to meet that demand. When I asked him what he believed was the number one rule of school, he quickly replied, "To listen." There is no dispute or disruption, no distraction or defiance. "You're supposed to just do everything," he explains. He understands what he is supposed to do yet behaves otherwise.

What might be learned from his willful defiance?

In his tireless quest for dispute, we learn that he values questioning. He refuses to simply accept things as they are; instead, he requires solid justification for the demands being made on him. He refuses the notion that because he is a child he deserves only marginal control over his activities, minimal freedom over his time. His constant questioning and the arguments and debates it causes reflect his insistence on being treated as a full human being with equal say.

I agree with Kate that questioning is a habit that helps people in life, however much it harms children in school. Knowing when and how to challenge authority is a skill worth teaching and learning. Understanding the power of organized, collective dispute—as an alternative to vulnerable, individual dispute—is also a lesson worth teaching and learning. Questioning is a habit we should cultivate in young people not because of its value to any particular individual, but because it makes for an undoubtedly healthier and more robust democracy. Democracy requires dispute.

Still, at school, Sean's individualistic approach to questioning is hurting him more than it is helping anyone. It is not yet strategic or reasoned, measured or balanced. His style is aggressive and it results in punishment. But school could value his questions. He could be actively taught to be more strategic about when and how he challenges authority. He could learn about historical figures that understood the power of collective action and organized non-compliance. He could be cultivated as a leader rather than punished as an outcast. In his commitment to willful dispute, I see the potential for the development of a feisty, tireless, politically active democratic citizen. But I fear the culture of school prevents such development by responding to his admittedly exhausting questioning with reprimands and redirection.

Schools claim to prepare children for a future in an imagined "real world." To teach and reward unquestioning cooperation is to maintain the status quo—preparation for a hierarchical social order of workers and bosses. By contrast, preparation for social change might instead recognize and celebrate the need for pesky and impassioned dispute.

If we listen to Sean's teaching, we hear the need for schools to instead cultivate in children the habit of strategic, informed, and collective questioning. As an individual Sean has the natural proclivity to question. He could be taught to adjust his tone, to learn the formal processes for making demands, including community organizing, written appeal, thoughtful debate. Literacy lessons for him might be framed through this lens and with this goal in mind—helping him understand literacy as power, helping him understand the role he might play as a citizen of the classroom community with a helpfully loud voice.

Importantly, framing Sean's willful dispute as an ingredient for potential leadership within the classroom might also address his overwhelming feelings of exclusion, his identity on the social margins of the classroom community, his heartbreaking sense that "nobody cares" about him. In light of these feelings, Sean leverages disruptive behavior as a way to be seen and heard, to feel that he matters.

Educators are often heard complaining that noncompliant children are "just trying to get attention." They often believe the right response is to ignore the child's attempts. I believe it's true that those who misbehave are often trying to get attention. Children, human as they are, require and thrive on attention—loving, generous, patient attention in which they feel seen, heard, and understood. But school is a crowded place, an increasingly sterile place, and too often a place in which children are expected to pay attention, not get attention.

In Sean's experience we see a problematic and unending cycle in which a child uses disruption to try to belong and be seen, and rather than recognize that basic human need, the common school response is to exclude him further—to send him away from the group repeatedly. The response is not particular to this school; I see the practice of exclusion and the withholding of attention in every school I visit.

The justification for such exclusion is that teachers do not want a child's disruptions to "distract" other children. In the individualistic culture of American schooling, it offends our sensibility to imagine that one child's disruption should be addressed as a problem of community rather than a problem in and of the individual. It seems inappropriate, of course, to allow Sean to impact the experience of his classmates. But Sean's willful disruption is a community problem because it is a response to community conditions. Feeling sad and left out, hurt and lonely, is a social problem that requires a social solution. Instead, exclusion is modeled by the school as a response, and then emulated by the children, who come to believe that Sean deserves to be left out. After all, they repeatedly witness his being sent away.

Instead of rearranging the culture of the community, the response is to isolate the problem in Sean. His shortcomings are cited and measured, beginning the process of urging his mother toward a medical evaluation. But, frankly, Sean misses a lot of academic instruction in the day-to-day. He often returns from taking a break confused about the task at hand and having missed the content required to successfully engage academic tasks. He runs out of time to complete assignments because he has been out of the room. This undoubtedly contributes to his academic shortcomings.

His social problems and physical altercations are cited and measured too, further pushing his mother toward considering a medical diagnosis. But, again, Sean does not have much opportunity to learn the skills of social relationship. The school day is highly structured and intensive, leaving children little time for play, for free conversation, and for unstructured interaction.

Sean is distracted, certainly. There is no doubt about that. But his insistence on willful distraction should draw attention to the lack of intentional time for healthy distraction in the school day—the need for breaks, for play, for movement, especially in spaces for young children. Teachers need this time, too. Even Emily, understandably, had tremendous difficulty sustaining her energy over the course of extremely rigorous and packed school days.

Sean's willful distractions can be seen as expressions of the human longing for social relationship. And they are a response to his desire to avoid feelings of sadness and loneliness. When the ADHD medication prevented these distractions, that sadness rose to the surface and made his deep loneliness painfully and heart-wrenchingly visible. Responding to his distractions with punishment rather than compassion is a mistake, however disruptive and inappropriate their manifestations. Sean teaches us to look for pain in the anger of children, to search for sadness in their outbursts, to respond with discipline, yes—but not with punishment.

Sean's defiance is indeed willful. And it is instructive. Sean defies the celebration of unquestioning obedience and raises the need for willful dispute. He defies the authority of the adult and honors the willful demands of the child. He defies invisibility by insisting on willful disruption. He defies boredom and control through the use of willful distraction. And perhaps most of all, in Sean's case, willful defiance is an expression of the human need for belonging and for community.

Marcus

On Being Good

"Is that coffee in there?" Marcus asks me, pointing to my cup and taking a sniff. It's my first time in his classroom and we have yet to be introduced. Morning circle is starting and all the kids are gathering. No other child has taken any interest in me, a stranger in their space. Marcus, by contrast, beelines right over in my direction and this is his first question. "Is it? I know it's coffee. Because I know white girls like to drink coffee. Why they like coffee so much?" He raises an eyebrow just enough to give away his attempt at provocation. I smile.

"I can't speak for white girls," I tell him. "But I like coffee in the morning because it helps me wake up."

"You tired?"

"No, because I have coffee."

"I need coffee."

"You tired?"

"Yes. I can't sleep good. I'm sleepy right now." Emily calls him over to the rug. He acknowledges her with a nod but makes no move. "Is that your computer?"

"Yes," I reply. I'm opening it up to start taking notes, and it becomes a source of great interest to him during our time together. "But Emily just called you over," I remind him.

"Yeah, I'm going. Did you buy that computer?" I see that Emily is waiting on him, and I worry about how disruptive I've been. I want to tread lightly on my first day. "I don't want to get in trouble," I tell him, being honest. "I'll talk to you later." He sucks his teeth and moves to the circle, pulling a chair up to the edge rather than sitting on the ground. It's an easy exit location, handy since he rarely lasts more than a few minutes in whole-group time. Kids are permitted to do this, and they are also allowed to stand along the edges if sitting is too difficult. Marcus always chooses a chair.

Marcus is charming, engaging, winsome. His eyes are a light hazel, almost green, and set against his light brown skin they seem to sparkle. He's round but not chubby—solid and strong. He gives great hugs.

He is usually in his black North Face fleece and sweatpants or jeans, and he alternates between two pairs of very clean, colorful, carefully maintained Nike high-tops. He steps a lot, to a beat, while moving around the room—and often claps a beat out as well. It's as if there is always a rhythm in his head and his body cannot help but move to it.

Marcus participates easily and enthusiastically in the morning circle game, but once that part of the routine is over, he gets antsy. A writing lesson starts and he begins making a beat on his legs while Emily is teaching. She is able to persist, though, and does. The other children manage not to be distracted. But now Maria catches his eye from across the room. She is at the take-a-break table in the back—the consequence of a transgression during morning circle.

She raises her eyebrows at him as if to say, *Join me*. No persuasion is necessary. Marcus gets up, leaves the circle, and begins to make his approach. Maria smiles in anticipation of his company. These two have a bit of their own routine. They like each other, often engaging each other in antics that tire the teacher out. But they also argue and fight like siblings.

Both are now missing the majority of the writing lesson. Marcus touches everything on his way to Maria's location, as if looking for a source of entertainment they might share—the markers, the timers, the computers. An eraser on Emily's desk catches his eye. He snatches it up and tosses it to Maria. A game of catch begins, subtle enough and far away enough from the lesson to go unpunished.

The two are very close to me, though. The eraser drops with a rubbery bounce and they look at me as if waiting for redirection. I acknowledge them but don't want to scold them or interfere. It's important that I not be a teacher figure in the space. Marcus mouths, "Can we play?" Even though it's my first day and they don't know me, as an adult I am assumed to have authority over their actions.

"I'm not a teacher," I respond. He shrugs his shoulders and throws the eraser to Maria. She misses the catch and the eraser hits my boot, landing directly under my chair. I make no move to retrieve it. Marcus is highly amused.

He goes over to Emily's desk, searches under stacks of paper, and finds a backup eraser. This time, as he tosses, he's aiming specifically for my boot. His aim is solid. It bounces right off the tip of my shoe on his first attempt. Impressed, I accidentally smile. "Marcus," says Emily from her spot at the front of the instructional area, "to the buddy room." The buddy room is a tier-two break option, an intermediary step between the time-out desk and the principal's office. A door connects Emily's classroom directly to a neighbor's, and Marcus goes through it. He is supposed to return when he is ready.

By the time Marcus reenters, the kids are knee-deep in their writing assignments, and having missed the lesson and the instructions, he is disoriented and disengaged. Emily goes right to him and offers him individual support to get him started. Multiple children seeking her help are turned away while she engages Marcus in the task. His pencil stops moving the moment Emily leaves him to tend to others. He balls up a small piece of paper and tosses it up and down until the writing time is over.

When Emily announces it is time for a read-aloud, Marcus grabs the bathroom pass and leaves the room. He misses the portion of the lesson in which Emily tells the children what they should be listening for as she reads. Her read-alouds are interactive, and these listening instructions orient the children to the comprehension strategy she is modeling and applying. When he arrives back they are already a few pages into the book.

Emily is reading *What Mary Jo Shared* by Janice May Udry, an old classic first published in 1966. Mary Jo's classmates are invited daily to share a prized possession, but Mary Jo is shy and afraid her classmates won't listen to her. Every time she gets an idea for something exciting to share, she becomes intimidated by how much better the other children's possessions seem to be. The book is highly regarded for being ahead of its time because it features a central black character, Mary Jo, while not being explicitly about race. Emily's book collection mirrors the makeup of her class demographics. Children can see themselves in the stories.

Marcus is playing with his shoelaces but seems to be listening to the story. He looks up from his shoe when Mary Jo's father comes home from work and asks his daughter if she shared today. "Not yet," replies Mary Jo, but then she gets an idea and asks her dad if he can come to school the next day. Her father agrees and Mary Jo seems strengthened, emboldened, ready to face her classmates and her shyness. I wonder how Marcus is receiving the book. His father is incarcerated. While his skin color is reflected in Mary Jo, his experience is not.

The next day at school Mary Jo shares her dad. She proudly tells her classmates all about his job—he is a high school math teacher—and their bond is obviously a special one. The children in the book respond with absolute delight, and they all want to share their own fathers with the class. Marcus cups his hands to his mouth and starts making loud bird noises as Emily is reading—chirps and tweets. They are eventually impossible to ignore. "Marcus," Emily begins gently. But before she can go on he makes his own choice to leave the rug. He goes to the back table to take a break. He sits, shuffles his feet vigorously for a while, and then lays his head down.

Moments later, while Emily is situating the other children with their instructions for independent work, Marcus gets up and loudly announces—in the silliest voice he can muster—that he's going to the bathroom, again. He says it several times and is obviously trying to be a visible and audible disruption. Emily is steadfast in getting through her directions, and she watches him leave the room while continuing her teaching. He returns with just as much hope of being noticed—loudly stomping his feet and dragging chairs along his path. "Marcus, come check in," says Emily, and she begins to walk toward him.

Marcus turns in the other direction, walking away from her as she approaches. She changes direction to follow. He quickens his pace. She quickens hers. In evasion and pursuit, they repeatedly stop, change direction, and speed up. Recognizing the dynamic, she says, "I'm not going to chase you around. We need to be able to have a conversation."

He stops. "I can hear you from here." He crosses his arms.

"That's too far. You need to be able to talk to me, Marcus."

"I. Can. Hear. You."

"If we can't have a conversation, I'm going to have to call the office." She takes one step toward him. He quickly moves away and sits at a table quite far from her. "Again, Marcus," she repeats. "We need to be able to talk." She doesn't move to him.

"You can come here if you wanna talk, then." He uses a challenging—almost threatening—tone. He is trying to be the one

to make the decisions, control the situation, undercut her authority. He mutters under his breath, "Nobody is the boss of Marcus
Andrews. *Nobody.*"

Emily takes a moment to gather herself, to figure out her next
move. The situation is public, challenging, meaningful. While she
is considering what to do, he quietly and angrily says, "We can talk.
Damn." And he pushes a chair, almost altogether knocking it over.
They're locked in the moment, the power dynamic. There isn't an
easy way out for either one.

Emily chooses to walk away, to steady herself and to recalibrate.
The stress level in the room is high, and at just that moment, a
child in another part of the room loudly complains about being
pinched. Emily, pushed far beyond her limit, uncharacteristically
loses her cool and raises her voice in response. I can't blame her.
We are all feeling the stress and the tension, the fatigue and the
frustration.

I can almost *see* the stress in Marcus's body—his shoulders
tense, his arms crossed, the loud and forceful stomping of his feet
against the floor. Emily is more sad than angry, and she continues
to pour her energy into the other children. She seems to decide
this is a way forward, and she begins to support other students
doing individual work. The kids appear to want to give her a break,
and several who are often difficult instead bring an unusual level
of focus to their tasks. This steadies her, and the attention away
from Marcus seems to steady him. The moment of tension slowly
dissolves, and Emily is able to celebrate the work of the children. I
see Marcus start to release the stress in his body. The more joyful
Emily seems, the more relaxed he becomes.

At this point, he has missed the majority of the academic
morning—both reading and writing. And because of the consistent hullabaloo, Emily has to postpone math. When she makes the
announcement, Marcus loudly cheers, "Yay!"

Both Emily and Marcus were getting support from folks at the school. The principal is not a behind-the-desk type by any means—active and informed, she is an instructional expert who was rarely found in her office and most often seen in the hallways greeting children and in classrooms working with teachers. She knew Marcus well and cared for him deeply, and she offered Emily a lot of support in the form of ideas, additional adults, and strategies. She was proud of the work Emily was doing, and she especially appreciated her strengths in teaching literacy. When I told her I needed a strong teacher for this project, she chose Emily.

The school was also staffed by a full-time counselor who was mentoring a counselor-in-training, so Marcus regularly received in-school therapy in addition to the whole-class lessons offered by the counselors. The counselor and the principal were often available to pull Marcus from class in urgent situations that required some relief for Emily. Because the schedule had Emily teaching for four hours straight without breaks each morning, this relief proved critical.

Out of school, too, Marcus was receiving support. Because the school's staff had such strong relationships with its families, they worked closely with Marcus's mother to support him in partnership. The school counselor referred the family to an outside therapist and also recommended that Marcus visit his father as often as possible. Despite an extremely rigorous schedule of work and home chores, his mother was diligent about following these recommendations. She took Marcus and his brother, a third grader, to see their dad twice a week—even though it meant not returning home until after nine p.m. on already hectic school nights. And despite also raising a teenage daughter and managing all the responsibilities of both home and full-time work as a bus driver, she never missed Marcus's appointments with the outside therapist.

With so much "support," though, Marcus's mother eventually grew wary of how many people were involved in trying to fix her son. "Everybody is always looking at him all the time," Cheryl told me as I tried to convince her to allow him to be part of my own research. "He's my child. I have to protect him. It's too much." At this point he was also being referred for special education services, so she was filling out multiple surveys and permission forms for various evaluations. All the while she felt as if her son was not improving. "I'm still getting calls all the time about how bad he is," she told me. She seemed so tired.

It is fair to say that Marcus's mother avoided me—and the suggestion of his involvement in this project—like the plague. Dozens of my phone calls went to voice mail. Multiple messages went unanswered. I understood her distrustfulness. She knew the people at school, but I was a relative stranger. The suggestion of a home visit, which was critical to my developing a fuller understanding of Marcus, signaled to her something akin to a child protective services intervention and accordingly she was deeply suspicious. It was hard to convince her that the project was a new way to look at Marcus, when it sounded to her so much like all the old ways: constant observation, scrutiny, data, a search for problems. It was hard to convince her that identifying pathology was not my goal. She was dubious.

I understood her fatigue. When she picked up my calls, I would learn that I was interrupting her late-night trips to the grocery store, her efforts to get dinner on the table, homework battles. She was busy, exhausted, and making it from one day to the next.

I hated adding to Cheryl's burden and often considered giving up. But I had already come to know Marcus from my time in his classroom, and I had already grown to love him. I looked forward to seeing him and I desperately wanted the chance to record and describe his extraordinary goodness—his charisma, his empathy, his smarts, his fierce love and loyalty.

Eventually, Cheryl agreed to talk to Marcus's father about the project and to make a decision about it together. When I met her for the first and only time at one of Marcus's outside therapy appointments, she agreed that his experiences were worth telling and gave me her permission. "But you have to actually help," she said, as a condition of his involvement. "You need to write up something soon about how to help him. A list of tips or something." I tried to explain that I didn't believe individual interventions—tips, as she called them—would do the trick. And I knew the school was already doing a million things by way of support for him as an individual. But she wouldn't hear it. He was going to summer camp soon and she was anxious that the people there would not necessarily try as hard as the school.

"You know things about him like what you told me, like how he needs breaks and he can't really stay still and how he's not bad," she insisted. "For the camp, you have to talk to them. Because I can't be getting phone calls all day long to come and get him." I agreed to what she was asking despite my hesitation. Her request reminded me of how slow and useless research can sometimes be to the people who most need a quick turnaround—the people who are struggling daily through the realities that researchers theorize about over many months and often years. Her situation was urgent and she did not intend to let me forget that. In fact, after meeting me that one time, she was suddenly the one with a sense of urgency. "Did you write something?" she would ask me in text messages. "Send me something," she pleaded.

I was never able to arrange a home visit for Marcus, or a long and formal interview with Cheryl. I was never able to sit down with him one-on-one outside of school, to hear his own perspective. I am lucky that he took such an interest in me and that he was so often willing to risk trouble in order to chat with me informally at school. He gave me much to learn and consider in those conversations. Still, in sharing his experiences I have had to rely more heavily on who he is at school. I do draw on my phone conversations with Cheryl and the one very important time I got to see Marcus with his sister and mother at the therapy appointment. My failure to see him at home routinely is a loss I lament, but his mother's distrust and hesitation about his involvement in this project, in and of itself, are important and informative. The distance she intentionally created matters, and it adds to the reality of the work schools need to do to earn the trust of families and communities.

The ferocity of Cheryl's instinct to protect Marcus was both palpable and admirable. She helped me to see who Marcus is at home, even though I couldn't witness those dynamics firsthand. Above all else, it is clear that he is a child who is loved, protected, and cherished.

Cheryl demanded that I provide her with a one-pager, which I did, offering four tips for supporting her son. The central story from the time I spent trying to comprehend Marcus's experience is his effort to reveal himself as good, to be recognized for that goodness—against and despite the consistency of his identification as bad.

Tip #1: Let Him Be Heard

Emily is starting reading workshop and Marcus pulls up a chair, as usual. She is reading *Wemberly Worried* by Kevin Henkes, and she asks the children to listen for a moment in the book where Wemberly's feelings change. "What are we listening for, Natalia?" She surprises a student to see if she knows the directions. Natalia shrugs.

"I know!" Marcus calls out. "I know what we're supposed to do." Emily allows him to tell her even though he has called out. She is giving him the chance to be heard, but within a narrow set of parameters around what he's allowed to say. (I think about this narrowness, too, when she pursues him in the hope of "a conversation." The way he moves away from her signals to me that he is doubtful an authentic conversation will take place; most likely he will be doing the listening while Emily does the talking.)

"We're supposed to say about a spot when, um . . ." He stumbles for a moment. Emily waits patiently and staves off the other students starting to try to beat him to the punch, hands frantically waving. "When he changes or something." Emily half rewards him since he half earned it, and again clarifies the directions.

"There are a lot of captions in this book, but I'm going to skip those for now." She begins reading.

Marcus listens quietly for a few pages, having caught the book from the beginning. But now he decides he wants to be heard. He interrupts, "Wait, read those little words—the, um, the caption things." I know Marcus heard Emily say she wasn't going to read the captions.

"He knows how to press my buttons," Emily later tells me. "I know his behavior isn't about me, but it's just so in your face. He's smart and he knows exactly how to poke me."

"Marcus, please." She continues to read.

He loses interest, and just remembering that he missed snack for a counseling appointment, he goes into his cubby and grabs his Doritos. He sits at the back corner of the room and begins to crunch. Crumbs are forming in a pile, which he diligently sweeps clean to the side, and then under the corner of the rug. He looks up to see if anyone is watching, sweeping with one hand and eating with the other. "What feelings did we hear?" Emily asks the children on the rug.

"Scared," one child offers.

"*No*—it's *scary*," Marcus interjects from the back of the room, mouth half full of Doritos. He is ignored. Emily writes *scared* on the easel.

"What else?"

"Sad," says another.

"What's a synonym for sad? A word that means the same thing but is stronger?"

"*Really* sad," Marcus offers, calling out once more. He smiles, as if to recognize that he has said something clever. He is again ignored. The kids continue to offer their thoughts, and he continues to add, correct, and override them from the back corner. "We already have that one up there," he says. "That's not even a good one." Emily finally puts her finger over her mouth and looks at him, signaling him to be quiet. "Excited. Frustrated. Happy." Now he's a loose cannon just shooting off distractions. Tell him to be quiet and he will increase his volume.

Emily looks at him for a long moment. He gets up to throw out his empty snack bag and grabs the pass for the hallway. "We can't wait to have you back, Marcus," Emily says to him on his way out, trying steadfastly to encourage him. Even I don't believe folks are looking forward to his return.

When he comes back Emily is talking to the children about expectations for their partner work time. She is reading a poster she made, which outlines those expectations. Marcus starts reading over her. "Okay. If people want to read, raise your hands," she offers. He raises his hand and she chooses him. She helps with some of the words and he gets through the entire poster. He is willing to be heard, under her prescribed conditions. But before she can celebrate him, he stands up and starts clapping out a beat, leaving the circle—now making himself heard on his own terms.

During partner time, rather than join his assigned partner, he walks over to the pair of girls sitting nearest to me. "You're gay," he says to one.

"She's a girl," says the other. "She can't be gay." Unfazed, they move forward in their work. His attempt to rile them has fallen flat.

Marcus then whispers to a nearby boy, and they crack up laughing. He looks at me. "Did you hear us?" he asks. Now I'm the object of his attempt to be provocative, to be heard.

"Were you hoping I would?" I respond. "Because if you want me to hear you, you probably shouldn't whisper."

"But people like secrets," he says. "They always wanna hear them. I coulda been saying something about you."

"If you're saying something about me, why would I want to hear it?"

"Why you think I said something messed up? 'Cause you heard me, right?"

"No. Because you whispered. If you had something nice to say, you could just say it."

"You mad?" he asks, and I can't tell if he hopes that I am.

"Mad about what? I didn't hear anything, so how could I be mad?" He palms his face, shakes his head, and walks away.

Being disruptive, provocative, and in-your-face are the strategies he uses to be heard. When he is physically present, Emily gives him multiple opportunities to be heard "positively," meaning within the parameters of acceptable student response, during lessons. "Marcus, I'm going to call on you to answer this question, so think hard. I believe in you. I want to hear your ideas." She means, specifically, that she wants to hear his ideas about the particular answer in question.

Sometimes he responds and sometimes he doesn't. I can't sense any rhyme or reason to those choices. But often he struggles to answer her questions, even with quite a bit of scaffolding. This isn't an arena where he feels confident, despite his generally strong academic skills. Whole-group lessons are public and fraught with emotional risk, and this isn't a way in which he cares to be heard.

Nevertheless, these are the terms of school. Children are heard only when they speak under certain circumstances—at the right time, on the right topic, when invited to speak. So Marcus is often silenced. Sometimes, in small ways, such as with a finger to a mouth in a *shhhh* signal, and sometimes in big ways, such as when he is removed from the space altogether for deciding to be heard on his own disruptive terms.

At the end of partner time, Emily sings, "Stop, look, and listen," to which the children are supposed to sing back, "Okay!" and turn in her direction with closed mouths. Marcus chooses to sing, "No way!" and laughs, heartily and loudly, with exaggerated drama. It is a public performance of his own creation, with the whole class as audience, and there is no ignoring it. In a smart turnabout, instead of saying "Okay," he is reversing the directive as if to say, *Stop, look, and listen—to me*. He is demanding that he be seen and heard, with all the inappropriateness he can muster so that nobody can manage to ignore him.

Emily sends him to the buddy room. When he returns not even five minutes later, he makes an entrance by walking *through* the children gathered on the rug during a lesson, knocking one out of her spot, and says, to the group, "What up, people? I'm back."

"You're not ready to be back," Emily says. No amount of time-outs ready him to be more quiet. Pretend not to hear him, and he speaks louder. Shut him out and he returns with renewed chutzpah.

"We've had a really good morning so far," Emily tells me one day when I arrive in the classroom. "But Marcus was sleeping." She laughs. "I hate to say it, but that was one less thing to deal with."

Short of being asleep, there isn't a way *not* to see or hear Marcus. Still, as much attention as he garners, I realize I don't know much about Marcus. I know he wants to be heard, and I consider suggesting that perhaps he be invited to share about something he feels expert about, a source of interest or knowledge. But I'm saddened to realize I have no idea what those topics might be. Classroom conversations are mainly about academic content. They invite children to be students and learners. But I wonder about a conversation that could invite them to be people, and also teachers. Knowing what Marcus might like to talk about would mean needing to know him as a person, but mostly I only get to know him as a troublemaker.

Emily tells me an important story about Marcus being heard that stays with me as I start to learn what matters to him: "There was one time—so, he got kicked out of the library all the time because it was Friday afternoon, and he was always at the end of his patience. One day, I guess what had happened is that he said something negative about hating books, hating to read books. And [the librarian] cares, and so she came down to talk to him. And she said 'I want to make the library a place you love. I want to make sure you love books. What can I do?' And I think he said he didn't have a lot of books at home. So she got a stack together to give him to take home, and it was the first time any of us had seen him have a smile—like a really real, genuine smile. Do you know what I mean? And it was like—it was such a nice moment. Because you get locked into this negativity, and I think we all needed to see that's what we want him to feel like. I just don't know how to help him feel that."

Sometimes it felt so complicated, knowing how to work with Marcus, how to lessen some of his negative behaviors. In moments like this it felt simple. It felt as if all he needed was an invitation to be heard on human terms. The conversation with the librarian was not a lecture, and there was not one clear response he was supposed to deliver—some form of acceptable or prescribed answers. She was open, ready to listen, curious, posing the problem and offering him the space to tell her what he might need. I doubt that his behavior in the library will improve because now he has books at home. But his behavior might improve because now he may feel that the librarian cares to listen to him—to let him be heard. An authentic relationship may be the only fuel on which Marcus can run.

Tip #2: Let Him Be Known

Marcus is lingering in the hallway before making his entrance to the classroom in the morning, walking especially slowly. "Good morning, Marcus," the principal greets him at the bottom of the stairs. "Hey, buddy," says the counselor with a smile as he passes. He waves to several older boys, who wave back, friends from the neighborhood. "Hi, honey," says the nurse. Marcus is always on time for school, and I'm glad he gets to experience the feeling of being known each morning. He doesn't smile much, but it's clear these greetings make him happy. The hallways are an enjoyable place where he will undoubtedly see some folks to meet and greet, so it doesn't surprise me that he often leaves class to wander them.

"Good morning, Marcus," Emily says when he arrives to her. "I'm glad to see you."

He waves at me, the only child to do so. "Got your coffee?" he asks.

"Yes, don't worry. I'm ready."

"I'm tired," he says. "What's that?" His attention is drawn to the background image on my computer screen.

"It's a picture I took of a spice market, in Cairo. My family is from Egypt. These are buckets of spices."

"That yellow stuff goes on food?"

"Yes."

"What is it?"

"I have no idea."

"Oh. Where you say you're from?" For a moment I forget who is studying whom. He's the one with all the questions.

"I was born in New York. But my family is from Egypt."

"Where's that?"

"Africa. At the very top. It's part of the Middle East. You heard of the Pyramids?"

"No." I pull up a photograph and show him. "Your family lives in there?!" His eyes widen. I laugh and slap my hand to my forehead. Before I can explain, the children are called to the rug. He makes no move, still awaiting my explanation.

"It's time for morning circle," I say with a tone that suggests our conversation is over. He nods and drags his chair to the circle to a spot nearest me.

As is typical, he plays the community game quite nicely. He has social skills enough to take turns, to be with others, to under-stand and respect competition—perhaps from his involvement in team sports. Other children are willing to play with him, and he is included fairly easily in games—both in class and out at recess. There are still many moments of conflict and argument with the other children, but generally these are times when he seems the happiest, and also the most successful and the most relaxed. Ban-ter is his forte. At the very least, these are the times he manages to stay in the classroom.

Relationships are key. "He loves people," his mother tells me. "He loves his brother. He's always looking out for him. Even though he's the younger one, he'll take anyone down for his brother."

Emily, too, describes Marcus as someone for whom relationships are valued. "He's charismatic," she says. "And also really loving. Like, my first thought about him at the beginning of the year is that he wanted to be known. He introduced himself to lots of different people at school. He wanted people to know him." His curiosity about me was in no way particular to me. If there is a new person in his space, he aims to know and be known. Indeed, on one of my days at his school, as I was grabbing my coat from the closet to get ready to leave just before lunch, he took my computer and held tight to it.

"You just got here," he said with a tone of accusation.

"No, I've been here for hours. All morning."

"What? You were here a short time, not a long time."

"Marcus," I begin, "I was here a long time. But you didn't see me that much because you kept leaving the room."

"Fine." He's annoyed, probably because it sounds like I am calling him out for his behavior—the kind of "conversation" to which he is all too accustomed. He puts my computer down on the table and walks away.

In his times leaving class he often goes across the hall, to his brother's classroom. He likes to visit with him. One particularly drama-filled day, he is drawn all the more to needing that relationship. It's his brother's birthday, and their teenage sister, a high school student, has stopped in unexpectedly to see the two boys. I assume she is here to wish Curtis a happy birthday, perhaps to join in his classroom birthday celebration. But she is crying and says good-bye to the boys in the hallway. They both hug her.

Marcus returns from the visit looking downtrodden, head hung. The children are writing persuasive letters, making a request and providing three reasons why their wish should be granted. Marcus sits down with a sheet of paper and a pencil but does not get started. Because Emily values independence so much, I am hesitant to go over and mobilize him, or even to talk to him. Her one request for me in her classroom was that I not serve as a "helper" because she did not want the children to grow accustomed to leaning on adults too heavily. I wanted to respect her request, but I watched as Marcus ramped up and started a conflict with the girl next to him, grabbing her pencil while she was trying to write. Emily was busy handling another student's needs, which were too urgent for her to manage both at once. I decided to go over and at least sit in between the children to stave off a fight until Emily was freed up.

"It's my brother's birthday," he tells me when I sit.

"I know," I reply, short because I don't want to be caught chatting him up.

"Did you type a lot today?" he asks. I don't respond. I am trying so hard to respect Emily's authority that I resort to ignoring him. I deny my own knowledge that he needs to be authentically heard. He starts again to mess with the girl's pencil, reaching across me to do so.

"We're writing letters," I say.

"I know." He reciprocates my shortness with shortness.

"You're not gonna write?"

"Nope."

"Why?"

"Nothing to say."

"You don't have anything you want that you can ask for in a letter?"

"Nope." Already we're in a teacher-student dynamic. I know he's thinking about his family and that he doesn't want to do this task—so far removed from where his mind and heart are right now. But I still feel the need to urge him forward in the work. I feel responsible for encouraging him to meet Emily's demands.

"Fine," I say. "But it's your brother's birthday. So you could at least write him a letter." And I get up to walk away. He grabs my shirt to pull me back down to the chair.

Dear Curtis, he begins to write. "We're going out to dinner," he tells me, looking up from his page. *I wish you a happy birthday*, he continues, *and where are we going today and we have to save food for Jada and Daddy and for me and you, too. From, Marcus.*

"Who's going?" I ask.

"Me and Mommy and Curtis." He starts to fold his paper up.

"So that's why you have to save food for the others?"

"Yeah, they're not there. Hey, do you know some people have two moms?"

"Yes," I reply.

"And two dads. Or no moms or no dads. Or just one moms or dads."

"Yes," I confirm. The counselor comes in and tells Emily she is going to take Marcus for a bit. Emily hesitates since he has missed so much of the instruction already, but she agrees. Minutes later, Marcus comes back in asking Emily if she has any plates.

Emily is confused. "What? Where are you?" Before he can explain, the counselor has returned to clarify. She's taking him to celebrate Curtis's birthday. Their mom is in the building as well, so the counselor wants him to join. Emily is annoyed. His academic day has been continually interrupted, and she has had to work multiple times to acclimate him to the classroom tasks upon his reentry. In addition, his behavior has been challenging all day, and now it feels as if he is earning an undeserved reward. "Marcus," she begins, but she seems to be speaking for the counselor's benefit as well, "you've missed most of the morning. When you get back, I need you to promise you're going to be in the room for the whole rest of the day." She explains at length why this is important. He stands obediently as she continues, not wanting to risk losing the privilege. I see his eyes quickly glance at the clock, likely wondering if he's missing the celebration as they speak. "I need you to do some work, Marcus," she starts to wrap up. "Because your brother has really been a distraction today." He nods.

"Do you have plates?" Emily and I both wonder if he has heard her, given how quickly he returns to his original focus.

"No," she says, and she turns back to work with the children on the other side of her. I worry about how much academic work he has missed today, too, but I also wonder if this is the day to take up that battle. "How is he supposed to be present in school when he has so much going on?" Emily asks me, rhetorically. I understand his family has been a "distraction" during this day, but the relationship he has with them is too central to be put aside for other activities—especially academic tasks that feel far removed from those relationships and those emotions.

It seems to me that school is the distraction from what he cares about, not the other way around. He works hard to make family at school, to know and to be known, to seek human relationship at every opportunity, no matter how rare. Because of the school day's central focus on academic rigor, there aren't many chances to be social. And he often misses play times to make up work or to take his licks for a transgression. The best opportunities for human connection are the ones he creates through his misbehavior—getting Emily's individual attention, visiting his brother, roaming the hallways, getting sent to the principal's office, being allowed to have private sessions with the counselor, feigning illness to go to the nurse.

I believe it would have helped Marcus to know Emily better as a person—as a human being rather than a teacher. His misbehavior allowed him more intimate time with her, but because that time was wrought with authority and consequence, she was forced into her identity as teacher all the more. She felt she couldn't let her guard down, that she had to hold him to high academic expectations and not allow his behavior to get him out of doing the work. Ironically, the more he sought her out as a person, the more she felt forced to behave like an authoritative teacher.

Tip #3: Let Him Be Helpful

Because Marcus values and thrives on relationship, he has an unusually strong sense of empathy for a child his age. I often felt as though his mood was calibrated by Emily's. When she was stressed, so was he. When she seemed joyful, he enjoyed her more. When it came to the emotional health of others, I felt he was the most attuned and the most compassionate community member in that classroom space. In this area, he could have been a leader. He had a natural and deep empathic stance. Maybe it was influenced by all that therapy, or in the value his family placed on care for one another. Maybe it's just his nature. Whatever the source of his strength in this area, Marcus really noticed how other people felt.

Still, while in fits of stress and upset, he was prone to actions that hurt people's feelings. The children were allowed to keep photographs of their loved ones in and around the classroom, and a few of these were posted around the room. In a bad mood one day, for a reason I never quite understood having missed the preceding events, Marcus tore Maria's family photograph almost completely down the middle. He had managed to stop himself before tearing it completely. Maria started to cry.

Jaelyn, her friend, comforted her briefly but then decided the best way to set things right would be to tell Emily and to bust Marcus. I expected Marcus's attention to be turned to Emily in an effort to somehow defend himself, but he chose a different response. "I'm sorry," he said under his breath, to nobody in particular. He went over to Emily's desk, grabbed her roll of tape, and started to patch the photograph up.

"I'm sorry, Maria." He made his apology sincerely and audibly and tried to hand her the repaired photograph. She continued to cry. "Here," he said, handing her the tape. "You can fix it more if you want." He returned to his seat and put his head down.

It didn't surprise me that he was saddened and remorseful. Maria was someone he actually had some semblance of an actual relationship with. And, of all the children, Marcus was the only one who seemed genuinely to care when other children were upset—no matter who it was. Three separate times I had seen him go over to comfort a crying child to whom nobody else was tending. One time, when a child was upset but he had to leave the room for counseling, he came to me and said, "Nyra's crying," as if to mobilize me to action. It bothered him when people did not get the help they seemed to need. And when he upset other children, which he did with some regularity, and if he believed he hadn't behaved well, he was remorseful and he made proper apologies without adult prompting.

I had seen Emily orchestrate *many* apologies between children, often forcefully and under threat of consequence. She had to coach them through taking responsibility, admitting wrongdoing, imagining how the other child felt, and setting things right. When Marcus transgressed, he knew it, and when he wanted to make amends he knew how. These were skills he had mastered.

It struck me, though, that when he was forced to make apologies he often resisted. On the particularly rough day in which he declared that "nobody is the boss of Marcus Andrews," the counselor came to get him to discuss the events. When they returned, she insisted he apologize to Emily.

"Go ahead," says the counselor. Her hand is on his shoulder and they are standing at Emily's side while she is supporting another boy with his work.

Marcus is silent. "No," he says.

"Marcus," the counselor begins, annoyed and disappointed.

"No," he says again, defiant. After all, nobody is the boss of Marcus Andrews.

"Then you're not ready to be back. And that's a shame because it's almost recess." Everyone here knows how to push buttons.

"I'm sorry," he says, muttering halfheartedly.

Emily had returned to helping the other child, upset about Marcus's refusal. When he makes his muttered apology, she puts her hand up to signal that she's busy and he should wait. Basically, she gives him the hand. He sucks his teeth. "Sorry," he says again, with a more aggressive tone, and he walks away. When Emily is freed up she goes over to talk to him. He folds his arms and turns away from her, standing still, waiting for it to be over.

Because I had seen Marcus make earnest and thoughtful apologies of his own volition on several occasions when he felt remorseful, I wondered why he refused this time. Perhaps he wasn't sorry. Or maybe he didn't like being forced—bossed around. With other children, apologies seemed easier for Marcus, perhaps because they were on a more equal footing in terms of power. Apologizing to a child didn't feel like being bossed; it felt like the right thing to do. But apologizing to Emily seemed to feel like giving in, handing over power, admitting that somebody *was* the boss of Marcus Andrews.

When Marcus behaved this way it was all the harder to make the argument that he craved the chance to be helpful. His actions were often so unhelpful to the smooth workings of the classroom. "I wanted to teach," Emily tells me. "But he just refused to cede the floor; he wanted to be the center of attention. So I couldn't teach."

Indeed, I felt that his battles with Emily were sometimes a competition for "the floor," the staging area. His performances seemed like a grab for power and attention, and I wondered whether having intentional opportunities for healthy, shared power and attention might prevent him from resorting to force. While other children ordered one another around and policed one another's behavior in their own efforts to be powerful, Marcus hardly ever did this. Sometimes he fought with them, but rarely did he try telling them what to do or regulating their actions. He focused his efforts on defying Emily, in particular, the clear authority figure. It was as if he felt that his peers were his comrades, but Emily was the force in power to reckon with.

He did like to be helped. The relationship Marcus sought with adults was consistently a helping one. He refused any dynamic in which an adult tried to exert power over him, instead insisting that the job of any older person was to help him—academically and emotionally. He was not willingly independent, and independence is a core principle of Emily's teaching. This conflict in their values caused tremendous difficulty. Marcus felt people should help each other and Emily felt people should be self-sufficient, to the largest degree possible.

Time after time, when Marcus's task was to turn his attention to academic work, he would scan the room for any adult he could lure into assisting him. There were often extra adults in the room. He felt they should be at his side. He rarely actually needed this help.

On the contrary, even despite missing so much class, his skills were strong enough to work independently the majority of the time.

On multiple occasions he tried to enlist my assistance with his work, but I steadfastly refused in order to honor Emily's focus on independence. "What are you here for if you never help nobody?" He used an accusatory tone. I was failing to meet his expectations about what an adult's role should be. He wanted that individual care and support. And he got it—from the counselor and her intern, from the principal, from the nurse, from his therapist. As his teacher, though, Emily saw herself as having a different role from those of these other adults. The others listened to Marcus, but Marcus's job was to listen to Emily. After an argument with her one day, Marcus announced angrily, "*Oh my god!* People never listen to people!" At his wit's end, he overturned a chair.

Emily was exceptional because of her particular insistence on independence. Though she worked with him individually and in small groups often, his requests for help from other adults were often a source of conflict. When he lured the counselor into sharpening his pencil for him one day, Emily was infuriated. "*No*, I'm sorry, Marcus. Give me that pencil." She took the pencil back to him. "There are sharp pencils all around the room and it is not okay for you to take advantage of people."

He tried all kinds of things to get adults to anchor him, to be at his side: pretending not to be able to spell words, insisting he didn't hear the directions (hard to refute, since he was so often out of the room), "losing" his pencils, purposely causing a commotion with kids around him so someone would have to come over. Emily sniffed out all his tricks and continued to insist on independence. Approaching me for help one day, he had barely made it within a few feet of me before she sensed his plan and redirected him: "Carla is closed. You know how to get started."

Ironically, as part of the result of the special education assessments at the end of the year, Marcus's individualized educational program included allowance for a full-time paraprofessional to be at his side in the upcoming academic year. He had to undergo the special education process, accepting the associated labels and diagnoses of pathology, to earn the relationship he had been fighting for all along. Still, there was concern that this person would be a crutch for Marcus, academically. I shared that worry, but I wondered when and how more authentic relationships might be forged for him at school without this support. I feared the paraprofessional would likely feel the same pressure that I had—to meet the demands of the classroom expectations rather than the demands of caring and genuine human interaction.

When a fifth-grade boy, Craig, spent the day in Emily's classroom because he could not attend his own class field trip, he became the primary object of Marcus's obsession. "You're here to help me?" he asked. Marcus aligned himself with Craig immediately, sitting next to him, chatting with him at every opportunity, grabbing him whenever it was time to work. He saw Craig as a leader, an older boy, and immediately figured the leader's role was to be helpful. Marcus left class much less often on this day, and I noted more effort to participate in lessons than on any other day I spent with him.

Amazingly, though, well acculturated to the nature of schooling, Craig took on a more authoritative teacher role with Marcus. He oscillated between helping him and bossing him. When Marcus's behavior would ramp up, Craig would clamp down in response. As Marcus lay down to rest on the rug during a lesson, Craig was immediately on him: "Get up, Marcus. What are you doing?" Craig's teacher talk was at the ready: "You have to try!" and "Why haven't you gotten started?" and, simply, "No, Marcus." Marcus lost interest in Craig before the clock struck ten a.m.

Feeling that the job of those in authority should be to help—not to boss—and wanting to align himself with authority at times, Marcus sought to give help as much as he sought to get it. On five

separate occasions, when Marcus was in class working with a partner, he simply did the work for the other person. "Here," he said to
his math partner, taking the workbook from his hands, filling in
the answers. "There. Now it's done. Here you go." The other boy
said not a word, looked at the page for a moment, closed the workbook, and moved on.

Marcus wanted this chance—the chance to be helpful, on his
terms. Emily's definition of *helpful* was for him to stop acting up,
to do his work, to be independent. But Marcus doesn't function as
an individual; he is fueled in and by relationship, in and by community. His definition of helpful is focused on others. Because he
rarely met Emily's standard of helpfulness, he wasn't given the opportunity to meet his own. There weren't chances for him to be
helpful on his own terms because he didn't earn those chances and
often didn't appear to be capable of them.

The most telling instance of his desire came toward the end of
the year, when Emily was trying out a system of earned points to
have him work toward a goal and earn a reward of his choice. He
was allowed to choose anything at all that he wanted as a prize to
work toward. Marcus asked to be allowed to help in the kindergarten classrooms. That was what he wanted. He didn't ask for more
recess time, for extra turns on the highly coveted iPad, which he
loved, for more choice, or for less work. What he wanted was the
chance to lead, to help, to feel what it is like to be good, to be in
caring relationship, to have a positive role in the lives of younger
others. He wanted to be a big brother, at school. His mother so
often celebrated him for his relationship with his older brother.
She felt that Marcus, despite being the younger of the two, was
the leader and the caretaker, the protector and the defender. She
thought this made him good, and he sought that feeling for himself
in school.

"He never earned it," Emily tells me. "He just couldn't get it together to earn the chance."

Tip #4: Let Him Make You Proud

I am meeting Marcus, his mother, and his sister at the therapist's office to get my final consent forms signed. School has now ended and I haven't seen Marcus in some weeks. I am really looking forward to greeting him.

When I catch sight of him, though, he seems far from pleased to see me. He hides behind his mom. "What is it, Marcus?" she asks, pulling him out from behind her. "You're not gonna say hi?" I tell him how glad I am to see him—the truth—but he is really not glad. I feel confused, and I start going over our last interactions in my mind.

"Don't worry about it," his mom tries to reassure me. "He had a bad day today and he's upset." She tells me camp has been rough, as she feared, and she had to leave work to pick him up early. She explains that they are starting medication—for anger and impulse control. "I don't wanna do it, but I just can't have these people calling me every day. I don't know. Maybe it can help." He moves away from us as we talk. He doesn't say a single word.

We sit a few minutes in the waiting area for the doctor to be ready. Cheryl tells me she wants to ask the therapist if I can come in and tell her about some of what I'm seeing at school. I'm not prepared to do this at all. "She doesn't get to be at school," Cheryl says, "so you need to tell her some things." I agree, since it's more an order than a request, and after they are in the appointment for a while she comes to get me and makes introductions with the therapist. But Cheryl positions me as someone from "school," and Marcus starts to cry.

In all my time at school I had never seen him cry. And this was not a few tears. This was a full-on, uncontrollable cry, the boy burying himself in his mother's side, trying to completely disappear into her hug. "Sometimes kids hear the word 'school' and they get to crying," said the therapist.

I believe Marcus thought I was going to say bad things about him. He thought I was going to reveal all the negative things, in detail, that happened in school—in front of his sister, his therapist, and, most important, his mother. His mom was already so disappointed about camp, so tired, so frustrated, so beaten down. The way he tried to hide in her hug seemed to me to be a way to beg her to just hold him, not to listen to anything I was about to say, to refuse the picture I was about to paint. I felt myself starting to cry too. I felt guilty and terrible for making him cry, but even more I felt heartbroken that he would think my picture of him would be an ugly one. On the contrary, I had not only an impression of his goodness, but also the data that captured it.

"Marcus, I wanted to tell your mom about some of the things I wrote down about you in school," I begin. He buries himself deeper. "I wrote down so many times I caught you being good." I expected to have to do a whole lot more talking before calming him down, and I wasn't even sure this would work at all—but I just didn't want to continue feeling awkward and responsible. Kids are smart enough to be distrustful, and adults always try to pretend they're going to say something nice when really they're going to follow the niceness up with something the child needs to improve upon. To my surprise, his sobs stopped—a small sign of trust. But he kept his face buried.

"Like the time when Nyra was crying and you were the only kid in the class who went to see if she was okay. Or the time you wrote Curtis that really good birthday letter, about saving food for the rest of your family. And when you were working with Emily at the back table and she gave you that super hard book, and you worked so, so hard to read all of it, and she was so proud of you. You smiled that time so I know you were proud of yourself, too. I wished your mom had been there because she would have been proud of you. That's why I wrote all that stuff down. So she could know about it. Your mom doesn't always get to hear about all that good stuff, right?"

Still uninterested in talking to me, or even looking at me, he did look up at his mom while I spoke about him. He unburied his face so he could see hers. It could not have been more obvious how deeply he wants to make her proud of him, how much he wants to be celebrated—not just in general, but by his mom in particular. He so rarely had the chance to shine for her, especially in the context of school.

In other contexts, though, he did shine and she could brag. She regularly complimented him as a brother. "He takes care of Curtis," she said to me in front of him. "He has his back. He cares about all of us. He's a good boy; he really is. "

He also shined in athletics, which made it all the more sad when he lost recess time—a time when he gets to be free, to be with other kids socially, and to be celebrated. At the end of the therapy appointment, Marcus asks his mom if they can stop to shoot hoops. Cheryl looks at her watch and agrees, with some hesitation. "Can she come?" He points in my direction.

In the elevator on the way out of the appointment, Marcus is looking and acting much more like his old self. We walk down the street to a house in the neighborhood, and his mom pushes open a gate that says, "No Trespassing." A play structure and basketball hoop are on the other side. They are obviously familiar with this spot.

Marcus's sister, mother, and I chat while he plays. He is climbing to the tippy top of the play structure and shooting hoops from there—but this requires that he hang precariously off the edge. I am sure he is going to fall to his death because I am of the nervous variety. I'm distracted, looking over in his direction a million times while Cheryl tries to talk to me. He knows he is scaring me, and he finds it delightful. He has my attention.

Because it takes work to get to the top of the structure, he doesn't want to have to come all the way down to retrieve the basketball each time he shoots. He elects his sister to help him, and she is generously passing it up to him each time. And each time he reaches out for the catch I try to block him from my peripheral vision so that when he falls, I am not witness to the tragedy. It is so difficult to make the shot with these acrobatics at play, but he is on a mission, and he wants all of our full attention so we can celebrate when he does. He repeatedly urges us to "look, look at me, look, I'm about to make it." And his mother does look each time.

"Aren't you scared to fall, Marcus?" I finally ask.

"Well," says his mom, "if he falls he will probably crack open his head or break his legs, and then we'll have to carry him to the hospital right up the street." She's being neither playful nor threatening; she's just stating the facts. "It's on you, Marcus."

"Look at me, Mama, 'cause I'm about to make it." He misses repeatedly and is starting to get upset. When his sister has had enough and decides to turn to her phone instead of retrieving the ball, his mom takes her spot as rebounder. No words are exchanged between them—it's just expected that they will help him meet his goal. As he's getting upset his mom is encouraging him.

"One of these times you're gonna make it," she says. "Just might not be today." I feel as if he's not worried about making the shot so much as he's worried about making her proud, giving her something to celebrate. With all the times she's forced to see him as bad, he seems desperate for the chance to show off some good.

Coda: Let Him Be Good

Many leading education scholars call for schools to center authentic and meaningful human relationships, empathy, and care between and among both teachers and young people. Marcus's demands echoed these most human of things—to be authentically heard, to be known, and to be celebrated. It's remarkable to see that a six-year-old offered the very same insights as highly trained and experienced "experts"—that fundamentally, care was more motivating than authority, reciprocal relationship more effective than power over, listening more useful than lecturing, healing more beneficial than punishment.

I never doubted that Emily cared about Marcus—she worried about him and wanted him to do well. She celebrated his small academic victories with much encouragement and joy. But Marcus was asking to be cared about as a person, not as a student. He wanted authentic human attention, not just academic interaction. He wanted to be known as a child, a brother, a full community member, and he wanted to be understood as a person who mattered.

I believe Marcus preferred the interactions with the counselors and the principal because their primary task was to hear him and to heal him. Certainly the reality of his situation at home was emotionally and physically taxing, and I often felt as though I could literally see the stress and fatigue moving through his body, preventing him from concentrating and sitting still. Both educators and more mainstream writers have begun to capture the relationship between stress and misbehavior, trauma and transgression—and the related need for schools to offer a healing rather than punishing approach to addressing noncompliance. Marcus was not able or willing to sit still and be quiet, fading into the background, compliant and focused on the academic work of school. This made him bad, however good his demands and his insights.

Though Marcus was calling for community and for care, the expression of that demand was extraordinarily disruptive, as Marcus chose outward defiance over more covert or nonconfrontational forms of disobedience. His transgressions were "in your face," as Emily aptly described them. It is significant that ultimately Marcus's therapist gave him medication to treat anger, rather than ADHD. He was just as hyper and unfocused, willful and prone to outbursts, as Sean, for example, but his acts were understood as the product of defiance rather than distractedness.

The "style" of his transgressions affected how they were interpreted. It matters that Marcus is a black male, and it matters that all the people with whom he interacts as "helpers" are white women. It is a problematic dynamic, these many white women working hard to heal and help him, and I often felt troubled by how much he seemed to crave their help. His desire for that particular kind of relationship in school bothered me because I felt it was still a position of subordination in which he was to somehow be rescued from himself.

But for Marcus, the alternative to this problematic dynamic was the relationship he had with Emily, which was fraught with power and authority issues. *Nobody is the boss of Marcus Andrews.* He never expressed any overt recognition of what it feels like to be a black male powered over by a white female, but the ferocity of his efforts to so consistently undercut her authority made me believe that he had a gut instinct about the need to alter the preestablished dynamic between them.

I do believe his disruptions were intended to defy authority. They served as performances in which, as Emily put it, he refused to "cede the floor" and he impeded her opportunities to teach. He used multiple forms of disruption to interrupt her. As Ann Arnett Ferguson, a researcher and scholar, writes, these kinds of performances "are strategies for positioning oneself in the center of the room in a face-off with the teacher, the most powerful person up to that moment."[13] Marcus wanted to share power. If Emily was going to sit in a chair on the rug, he was going to sit in a chair on the rug. If Emily was going to make people, "stop, look, and listen" to her whenever she felt the need, then he, too, would show his ability and power to force the group to pay attention to him. As Ferguson explains:

Fundamental to the performance is engagement with power; authority is teased, challenged, even occasionally toppled from its secure heights for brief moments. Children-generated theatrics allow the teasing challenge of adult power that can expose its chinks and weaknesses. The staged moments heighten tension, test limits, vent emotions, perform acts of courage.[14]

This toppling of authority is considered "oppositional" because it opposes the norm of what is expected—that children automatically be subordinate to adults in school. This kind of subordination takes on particular meaning when it intersects with race, gender, and class. A white middle-class girl as subordinate to a white middle-class woman has a different symbolic and historic tenor to it—a less loaded and fraught one—than the dynamic of the subordination of black working-class males to white middle-class women. It cannot be ignored, even if the black male is barely seven years old. He is still fully human at the age of six, and he still has the capacity to exercise his right to oppose subordination.

Marcus's opposition was interpreted as anger—a personality disorder rather than a commentary on the way power and subordination work in the world, and in the classroom. In reality, I do think he was angry. I, too, become angry when people act as though they matter more than me—as though we are not equally human and equally powerful.

Official power at the top is not the only kind of power. There is power, too, that springs from the "bottom," and as much power as Emily had to talk, Marcus had equal power to interrupt her. He recognized that power and he asserted it, regardless of the consequences. Already labeled a troublemaker, he had little to lose as he engaged his own identity work as a person equally deserving of being seen and heard.

Reframing the interpretation of Marcus's transgressions can help disrupt his identity as "bad." Ultimately, though highly inappropriate and disruptive in his delivery, he was insisting that power be shared in the classroom, that everyone have an equal right to be seen and to be heard. He was asking for relationships in school that mirror the relationships modeled at home—care and commitment regardless of how much "trouble" someone is in. He was calling for children to have a voice and to make contributions on their own terms, not just in narrow academic terms, with adults who were able to be more open and curious about their opinions, ideas, and experiences as people rather than just students. His demands were such very, very good ones—if only people could let him be good.

Conclusion

Trouble-Making in School

If we saw these four children only in school, we might not be able to see them as anything but troublemakers. In school, they are exhausting and tireless, frustrating and challenging. This school identity can seem to be their only identity if we fail to account for who they are in the many other parts of their lives—daughters and sons, martial artists and basketball players, poets and artists, experts and natural learners. The voices of the families in this book—mothers describing their precious and fragile babies in utero, recalling their toddlers' earliest triumphs and struggles, flipping through the photo albums of their most human memories—paint alternate pictures of their children for us to view with reverence and delight.

These alternate images allow us to view children as complex and beautiful human beings rather than caricatures of troublemakers. Their humanness encourages us to try to understand their difficult behavior through a more generous lens—a lens that treats *trouble-making* as a verb rather than a noun. As a noun, a troublemaker is a kind of person—an identity encoded in and imprinted on individual bodies. It locates the problem of noncompliance in people, fogging our view of the social and cultural production of trouble. By contrast, we can instead treat *trouble-making* as a verb—a process, an action, a system. We can ask, How does trouble get made as these children interact with school? Such a question redirects our attention away from "fixing" people whom we assume to be broken and instead toward addressing the harms that seek to break them.

Schools are a particularly harmful institution for young people. Trouble gets made because schools engender it, exclude it, and ultimately work hard to simply erase it. Schools try to make trouble invisible, most often by attempting to eliminate the young people who are working so hard to make it visible.

Schools *engender* trouble by using systems of reward and punishment to create a certain kind of person—"a good student"—a person suited for the culture of schooling. Good students sit still; they listen; they follow directions; they conform; they take orders; they adhere to the terms and standards of childhood as a marginal social position and to whiteness as the ideal. Students do well in school and will be counted as good when they allow others to exercise power over them.

Those who resist this narrow definition of what it means to be good are *excluded* from the community of goodness more broadly. Rejecting the identity of "good student" does not mean that children get to select their own identity in the image of freedom. Instead, failure to achieve identification as a good student means the default assignment of an alternate school identity—that of troublemaker. Exclusion is a way to cement the identity of a child as a troublemaker, relegating her or him to the outskirts of the "good" classroom community. These children become outcasts; marginalization is the punishment for refusing to conform to the mainstream.

By excluding trouble, schools hope to *erase* it. Schools gain their legitimacy from the appearance of goodness, from the willingness of their students to behave well, to work well, to score well. The hope is to eliminate noncompliance, to make misbehavior disappear, and this requires that "problem children" themselves be rendered invisible. That invisibility can be seen in the experiences of these four children, even as each child goes out of her or his way to be extraordinarily visible.

When considering how schools participate in making trouble—how they engender trouble, exclude it, and try to erase it—I do not mean to indict the particular schools or teachers featured in this book. On the contrary, I purposely chose schools that are highly regarded, that have strong relationships with families and with the communities they serve, and that aim to be progressive and creative, compassionate, justice oriented and inclusive, steadfast in their mission to serve all children. It is important to understand how children struggle even in these schools because it demonstrates the systemic, cultural, and often invisible workings of *school*, as an institution.

School is generally understood to deliver instructional content to children, arming them with the knowledge and competencies required for a future in the job market. Teachers often believe this work is neutral, shaped by objective standards rather than subjective values. But schools *make* people. In the everyday work of classrooms, social identities are fomented and cemented in the minds and bodies of young people. This is active political work, cultural work—not neutral, passive work.

Rules, and the rewards and punishments used to legitimize and enforce them, are the central means through which people get made in school. Disciplinary practices make the extreme regulation of bodies, the dominating power of the authority over the docile, appear normal and natural. "Classroom management" seems a neutral and harmless phrase. But the management of classrooms requires the management of children—which means power over people, control over bodies. These efforts cannot possibly be neutral or harmless. In classrooms human beings are told how they will line up and walk, when they will be permitted to use the bathroom, to eat, to speak, to sit down or to stand up. Such stringent limits on human freedom are bound to be fraught with trouble.

School rules are used to create the bounds and borders of acceptability. They encode morality and value systems, and they define the parameters of goodness and badness. Children who follow the rules get to be a certain kind of person—a good person, a successful student, a fully included member of the classroom community. Children who fail to follow the rules get flagged, punished, diagnosed, remediated. They get to be another kind of person—a bad person, a failing student, a problem child, a marginalized member of the classroom community.

No child is naturally a troublemaker. A child is who she is—and when she walks through the school doors and interacts with its arrangements and rules, its requirements and demands, she may find herself in trouble if she challenges and refuses the power of the school to make her into a conforming, self-regulating, and self-disciplining person. It is in this interaction between child and school that trouble is made.

Consider Zora. Visiting her at home, I see the inspiration for much of Zora's out-standing-ness. Opening the door of her rainbow-painted gate, taking a tour of her wild and overgrown garden, breaking bread at the dining table into which her mother has etched flowers and vines, I see the seeds of her creative spark as a maker and a dreamer. Of course she won't just cut out some animal picture and glue it onto a folder, no matter what kind of authority tells her to do so. She will instead search high and low, in piles upon piles, for a collection of birds she can perch upon the shoulders of clay royalty.

Reading the Spanish word labels everywhere in her home, the inspirational quotes and posters from African American leaders that adorn her walls, I see that her parents are powerfully drawing attention to her blackness, her Puerto Rican–ness, even as her color sets her apart from nearly every other child at her school. Zora's parents are actively teaching her to stand out, to be bold, to be different, to take pride. These are strategies and ways of being that have allowed them to thrive as folks of color in white spaces, and they pass this wisdom on to Zora with clarity and intention. They want her to remember who she is because the supremacy of whiteness functions to try to make her forget.[15]

The person Zora is encouraged to be at home is discouraged at school. Mrs. Beverly and Mrs. Norbert never claim to be neutral in their efforts to make people. They are explicit about the fact that there is a "white-bread Americana" school culture, and they are insistent that every child get acculturated into it. They believe it is their duty to teach kids to do school—and they will "fight the fight" with children who resist. They teach kids to walk a certain way, to hold their arms a certain way, to grip their pencils a certain way, to speak a certain way—in short, to *be* a certain way. Children are regularly made to practice these ways of being, and they are publicly rewarded, or redirected, for successes and missteps.

Mrs. Beverly repeatedly says she doesn't want Zora "to stand out," that she wants her to learn to regulate and discipline herself so that she goes unnoticed. She fears that Zora already stands out as one of the few kids of color, and she wants her to fit in, to conform. Zora is too different—loud, active, unruly, bossy, noncompliant. Of course, her parents don't necessarily find these qualities problematic. Indeed, these are qualities often associated with leadership and with groundbreaking boldness. But at school, the identity required is more conforming and constrained. You shouldn't be noticed at school.

Ironically, Mrs. Beverly shares some of Zora's characteristics. Like Zora, she is unique. She, too, stands out, with her tall frame, her bold color combinations, her eccentric accessories, and her loud voice. Like Zora, she is full of rebellious conviction. She refuses to comply with directives from above if they fundamentally challenge her own beliefs. Her feistiness is intimidating to administrators, and she is at the ready with her résumé should they choose to overstep with their challenges. She and Zora have much in common—two wild peas in a constrained and constraining pod. But the classroom is too small to permit the authority of the both of them. Mrs. Beverly responds to a challenge by stepping up times two, not backing down by half. So Zora needs to stand down, to fit in, to do as she is asked.

Yet, Zora is who she is. She is out-standing. Her parents celebrate it, but at school, it makes trouble.

Lucas, too, is who he is. He is perseverating and inflexible. He delights in freedom and fun, and he experiences his own needs and desires as urgent. Sharing space with twenty-five children is going to be a challenge for a child who could not share space in the womb with his twin brother. Lucas is just the kind of person to sit on a neck if it means a more comfortable position for himself. He's not selfish or cruel; he just struggles with the empathy and foresight required to respect and appreciate the needs of others. He is wacky and hasty and hilarious and he likes a good time and needs a good laugh. The seriousness of school is dulling to him, and the rigor and the rushed schedule cramp his style.

Unlike Zora's mom and dad, Lucas's parents are not actively teaching him to be a different person than the school seems to value. On the contrary, they agree with the school's assessment that some of his qualities are problematic and are trying to curb those aspects of who he is—including rewards and punishment at home, as well as medication to assist him in conforming more easily to a particular social world. But his mother acknowledges that sometimes he just needs some time and space to be who he is. She disciplines him, certainly, but she also builds in some accommodations to make room for him as he is.

"He needs some time to just *be*," she says, explaining that at the end of the school day he is often so spent that she gives in to some quiet time for him rather than drag him to the organized activities his siblings happily engage in. "I find that when he comes home from school he needs that time," she says. "Like a lot of times he'll take his Kindle, and I'll look down the hallway, and he's lying on his bed, playing with his Kindle, or he's playing a Sonic game, or something like that on it. Or watching a video on it—a Sonic video. But I find that he does need that chill time. Even though we've been trying to curb the electronics, sometimes I stretch out that time for him."

Who Lucas is conflicts with the kind of person required by the school. He is choice-loving, not obedient, and he is much too inflexible to meet the many rigid, imposed demands of schools. He benefits from a classroom that is mixed age, highly engaging, active, and organized around stations and rich, creative units of study—and from a veteran teacher who has experience enough to handle him. But even in this progressive space he struggles. I worry about how much more trouble will get made as he travels through the grades into classrooms that will be increasingly traditional, rigid, and unforgiving. The qualities he brings to school are just not well suited for its demands.

Trouble gets engendered in Sean's experience of school because he is pesky, argumentative, tireless, and willful in his disputes and his demands. He requires explanations, he challenges authority, and he negotiates for his own desires at every turn. What his mother calls "questioning," his teacher describes as "badgering." His mother likes who he is. She takes him seriously as a full person with an opinion that counts. She hears him out and she shares power. This is possible in a household of two, as opposed to a classroom of twenty-five. It is also possible when your goal is to raise one child rather than to "manage" a crowded and chaotic mass of children. Kate believes his refusal to roll over, his refusal to be powered over, will help him in life. But she readily concedes that it will not help him in school. School requires a different kind of person from Sean—a more agreeable kind of person, a person who accepts directives without a fight and without negotiation.

To Kate, Sean is boyish and active and energetic—normal. To the school, Sean is impulsive and disruptive—difficult. The person he is encouraged to be at home is not a person who will do well at school.

And, finally, Marcus is his own person. While school is increasingly about the sterility of standardization, Marcus is steadfastly fueled by the humanness of social relationship. He insists on being cared for, on being known, on being valued and heard. And, however disruptively and inappropriately, he is calling on the school to recognize and celebrate him as a person, not just a student.

Marcus rejects the framing of the teacher-student relationship as a dynamic of adult power over child. He reframes the relationship as one in which older folks are supposed to help and support young folks. This community model of care is central to the way his family works, and "having each other's backs" is central to his mother's pride in her children.

In keeping with the emphasis placed on care, the presence of Marcus's father despite his incarceration is important. No matter how socially excluded his father may be, however strong his father's own assigned troublemaker identity is, the family's recognition that he matters is unwavering. Their regular visits, his presence in Marcus's world despite his absence, the way Marcus's mother made a point to include his father in the decision about whether to allow Marcus's participation in this project—all reflect a steadfast insistence on Marcus's dad's value as an important family member and as a person deserving of inclusion. Marcus has learned to always—*always*—save food for his dad.

The value placed on individual success at school directly conflicts with the value Marcus places on community, as does the regular practice of exclusion as a response to transgression. While Emily deeply values independence, in keeping with school culture, Marcus deeply values interdependence and inclusion. He is, nevertheless, frequently misheard and misunderstood. Insisting on community and human relationship, he is ironically accused of disrupting community, on harming relationship, on threatening the possibility of peace in the classroom. He wants people to help each other, to hear each other, to care when someone is crying and to worry when someone is excluded. But his troublemaker identity is so overpowering that it renders his fundamental humanness invisible. It looks as if he is only trying to get attention for himself, to have his own needs selfishly met, when really he is actively drawing attention to the basic human needs of others.

School is trying to make people, but these young people insist they are already made. Their families, their communities, their histories, their biology, their preferences, make these children distinctive people already—people with ways of being that happen to be misunderstood, undervalued, and ultimately unwelcome in school.

Families may model, teach, and value ways of being that they consider not only unproblematic, but actively healthy—like Zora learning to be unique and proud, Sean learning to question and argue, Lucas craving choice and freedom, and Marcus choosing *not* to be independent. But these ways of being sometimes get systematically punished by school. It is amazing, and disturbing, how early this process begins. These children have barely been alive seven years and already they have been identified as problems.

All four children were medicated before the end of our time together. It is increasingly routine and shockingly acceptable to drug the fragile, developing brains and bodies of young children into compliance and docility. The extent of our willingness to change children, coupled with the extent of our unwillingness to change schools, must awaken our collective moral conscience toward a new imagination and approach.

The children's early refusal to trade their own identities for more acceptable, "good" ones, and the resulting assignment of an identity as *troublemaker*, make the school's uncompromising demand for more conforming and cooperative identities visible to us. Having engendered trouble—creating the parameters of goodness and badness—schools must then work hard to exclude it, rejecting those who fall outside of the bounds of goodness. There are significant consequences for getting in trouble, for being a problem. Both academically and socially, the central consequence is exclusion—exclusion from class, but more important to these children, exclusion from community.

All four of these kids were willing to transgress, to break rules and cause disruptions, despite the risk to their relationship with the teacher and the punishment that would undoubtedly be handed down. Zora, Lucas, Sean, and Marcus all endured individual punishments in order to get a laugh, acceptance, or other affirmation from their peers.

Zora regularly used drama and slapstick humor to take center stage and entertain the group. She was willing to call out if she had a good enough joke, even knowing Mrs. Beverly never let things slide. She didn't mind distracting others in small-group work to have a little shared fun, even if being off task meant making up the work during a free time. These were the only times she really had the attention of other children; even if that attention turned negative, it was worth the chance of earning even one moment of belonging. Lonely on the margins of social classroom life, and in a push-pull dynamic with the one "friend" she found in Tyler, she too often found herself alone and was willing to risk punishment to earn some sense of social acceptance.

Similarly, Lucas offered multiple examples of clowning. At the Native American station, he was willing to mock the tribal elder in the video for a laugh, despite the fact that Mrs. Norbert would absolutely never stand for that offense. On the playground, his "toilet humor" went a long way toward getting laughter, despite being strictly forbidden. And he often got busted for conflicts with Stella in his fight for sole custody of Sam. Making and securing friends were often the goals of his antics, despite the risks involved.

Sean's obsession with Ilan, who also found great entertainment in naughtiness, cost him many a punishment when it came to Emily. He caused many disruptions during class, especially when all of the kids were gathered as audience—kissing jokes, inappropriate sound effects—and often very obviously scanned the group for hints of affirmation for his antics. Aggravating Emily and setting the academics off course did not seem consequential to him.

Marcus was slightly different from the others in that he was generally fairly accepted by his peers. They fought with him often, as they did with one another, but on the whole they were willing to be with him and play with him. Still, as with the other children, want of attention and approval fueled many of his disruptions—his shouts of "What's up, people?!" and his shenanigans and even his whispered insults and provocations suggested the desire to be seen and heard. Like that of the other children, his misbehavior won him the chance to know and be known—by adults and children alike.

These children risked punishment, risked their relationships with the teacher, to carve out a thread of belonging in the social fabric of the classroom. Assigned troublemaker identities, they worked within those identities to do this work of attempted inclusion. At the same time, the more they misbehaved to earn a place in the community, the more they were excluded from the community.

Teachers felt that these children threatened the community, disrupted it, ruined it for the other children. As Jeff Duncan-Andrade writes about putting young people out, "We rationalize the exclusion by telling ourselves that we have pulled a weed from our garden, allowing for a healthier environment for the other children to grow."[16] When Emily tried to build community through morning games, Sean ruined them for everybody by refusing to wait his turn and play by the rules. When she tried reading a beloved story aloud, Marcus interrupted so many times that she lost her joy and the children lost their opportunity to share that joy. So she plucked the weeds—she sent Sean and Marcus to the back, or to the room next door, or to the counselor or to the principal. Eventually Sean got sent to the doctor and Marcus to a special education evaluation. Perhaps with these weeds plucked, the other children who *did* follow the rules and *did not* ruin things for others could enjoy a game, a book, a place in the classroom community.

But despite the attempted removal of the weeds, this hope of a community never formed. "I just couldn't build the community I am usually able to build," Emily lamented. Her disappointment was palpable.

One reason for this is that exclusion does not build community—it destroys it. The problem with weeds is that when you pull up one, many more sprout with a vengeance. It isn't the behavior of the children that threatens community; it is the response to that behavior, the use of exclusion, that threatens community.

When a child is excluded, it teaches the other children that belonging to the classroom community is conditional, not absolute, contingent upon their willingness and ability to be a certain kind of person. In this paradigm, belonging is a privilege to be earned by docility, not a basic human right that is ensured for every child.

Duncan-Andrade reminds us that, in the words of one educator, the students are all "indigenous" to the classroom and therefore "there are no weeds in my classroom." The young people are indigenous because they are the natural part of the school community. They are indigenous to the neighborhood to which the school belongs, and they are indigenous to the culture of childhood that dominates the classroom.

Given the realities of school segregation and the demographics of the teaching profession, young people have much more in common with one another—culturally, socioeconomically, linguistically, developmentally—than they do with their teachers. The young people comprise the community. The teachers are the interlopers, the outsiders, the ones who come and go, the ones who don't fundamentally belong. The children are a community garden long before the teacher arrives on the scene with her own outsider tools, so when she pulls a "weed" she disrupts the balance of community by creating the threat that any child, at any time, can be excluded at her will. She leverages power and authority to show that she is the ultimate arbiter of community belonging.

This creates a sense of danger, a feeling of warning, a lack of security. The use of public exclusion is a way to cement the docility of the other children and to ensure the teacher's absolute right to decide who gets to belong and who doesn't. Sometimes teachers even mobilize the children to help police the bounds of community. Mrs. Beverly, for example, often used public reprimands as a means of teaching and learning for the audience of children bearing witness. "If I'm scolding someone," she says, "I'm not necessarily scolding in a quiet voice." She goes on: "I scold out loud so that everyone hears the message. And I think that's something that has sort of gone by the wayside in this misplaced notion that kids need to hear about misbehavior in a quiet way. I find that this classroom functions pretty well, and kids know each other's business in a way. Not in a mean way, but in a way that—like, I've asked the class before, 'Look, here's someone who is having a really hard time calling out. Use the signal, do a reminder, and that's going to help this person be able to function in our world.'"

The children are being taught that calling out is not a way to "function in our world." Belonging in "our" world—a white world, that is—requires a certain kind of behavior, and the children are given explicit permission to share her authority over one another, to police one another. This is framed as helpful. Mrs. Beverly believes she is empowering children to take control over their community space, to share responsibility for making it function well. This feels to her like building and maintaining a community. In her view, she is not imposing her will; the community is policing itself.

But what actually happens when the children give Zora and Lucas obnoxious quiet signals and remind them in authoritative tones, modeled by the teachers, not to call out? What dynamic is created for Zora, especially, when a bunch of white children police one of a very few children of color, with the authority of the white teacher vested in them?

With every reprimand, every public scolding from teachers and children alike, Zora and Lucas get pushed further and further to the outskirts of the community. This doesn't help them function in "our" world; rather, it further reminds them they don't belong to that world. They are outcasts. And even though Mrs. Beverly and Mrs. Norbert never send kids out of the room—on the contrary, they insist on keeping them in the classroom at all times—they still manage to use exclusion as a way to regulate misbehavior. Zora and Lucas do not belong, and they are lonely and left out. They are excluded from the community of goodness and docility. You don't have to physically put a kid out to exclude him. And all the while the children are blamed for their own exclusion because the problem is located in their behavior rather than in the school's response to that behavior.

These four children tirelessly undercut the authority of the teacher to dictate belonging in the community. They use disruption to threaten the teacher's control over the community, while simultaneously leveraging their antics in the hope of making the children accept them despite their constant marginalization.

Getting in trouble is worth the risk if the result is a momentary sense of belonging, some fleeting relief from the deep loneliness of being different and being left out.

From these children's misbehavior, we learn that young people do not lightly accept being treated like weeds—ugly discards. They refuse to be kept at bay, poisoned, or plucked. They refuse to be made to disappear.

The more the children were rendered *invisible* by their schools—either by trying to force them into conformity or by completely ignoring their efforts to be noticed—the more they responded by making themselves *hypervisible*.[17] In the stories of each of these four children, invisibility and hypervisibility work as a sort of perpetual cycle of cause and effect—a chicken-and-egg situation where it is impossible to know which came first. These four children worked very hard to be seen and heard. They made themselves hypervisible through a multitude of strategies of disruption and performance. In response, the teachers worked doubly hard to quiet those disruptions, to make the kids more "normal" and less noticeable, to wall out their blatant requests for attention. And again feeling unseen, the children increased their efforts to be seen through outrageous transgressions.

Zora made herself stand out. She moved around when she was supposed to be sitting down; she called out when she was supposed to be listening. Tasked with making quiet, serious, and scientific observations of moths, she chose instead to create loud, silly, and distracting performances of people face-to-face with bugs. Assigned to glue animal cutouts to her folder, she instead set a paper seagull in motion through the classroom air, allowing it to pretend poop on a classmate's shoulder. When the cafeteria rule is to take only one straw, she grabs ten so she can create a super straw and launch spitballs. She is loud, active, and dramatic. She makes herself seen.

Lucas, too, draws attention to himself by doing what he wants as if no rules, no codes, and no other people exist. He gets up in the middle of a read-aloud to pursue a book of his own choosing on the other side of the room. He smashes another child's Lego creation to bits in order to satisfy the needs of his own plastic dinosaur, which "needed something to attack." When he complains about intruders at his lunch table and nobody does anything about it, he stands up in the middle of the cafeteria and repeatedly, forcefully kicks the trash can. He makes himself seen.

These efforts to be seen were considered inappropriate and the teachers felt their job was to stop them, to squelch them, to train the children to be less visible—more quiet, more still, more compliant, more conforming. The teachers felt they were preparing the children for the reality of the way the world works, for subsequent grades and for life. "The expectation as they go on is going to be that you will raise your hand, you will wait, you will do your work," says Mrs. Beverly. She felt it was her primary responsibility to make their behavior "commensurate with the expectations of the classroom" and with the middle-class white world of work. And these expectations included not standing out in ways considered strange or different. They would not permit hypervisibility. At every turn, they aimed to blend children into the crowd—to make them less visible.

They tried to erase trouble by making difference invisible.

For Emily, making misbehavior disappear sometimes meant pretending the children themselves were invisible. Often the children were literally ignored, even (or especially) when they were engaging in highly audible, highly visible, outrageous disruptions. Sometimes it amazed me how Emily, and the other children, were able to persist through a lesson or activity despite Sean's and Marcus's efforts to divert the academics in favor of their antics.

When Sean enacted his willful disruptions, every effort was made not to reward his mischief with the attention he so desperately worked to attract. When the children were repeating a book refrain joyfully, in unison, he interrupted their choral reading with a *"Let's party!"* It's not like anyone didn't hear him—it's impossible not to hear him. But nobody reacted—neither Emily nor a single child. Nobody even looked in his direction. For a moment I wondered if I had imagined it. His disruptions had become so routine that nobody bothered to notice them anymore. This required him to step them up tenfold, which he did. He got up, walked through and over children seated in his way, and stood directly in front of the book, making it impossible to treat him as invisible. This dynamic happened on multiple occasions.

Similarly, when Marcus calls out adjectives from the back of the room while eating his Doritos, aiming to attract attention away from Emily's literacy lesson, he is repeatedly ignored. When Emily puts her finger to her mouth to signal him to be quiet, he yells louder. When he chirps and tweets during the read-aloud of *What Mary Jo Shared*, trying hard to interrupt the story, he is ignored until he raises the volume so high as to make it impossible to shut him out.

Feeling invisible—unheard, unseen, unrecognized—made the children more fiercely insist on drawing attention to themselves. But, of course, their efforts were often wildly inappropriate, ensuring that nobody could possibly pretend not to see them.

What do we learn from the children's refusal to be unseen and unheard? Centrally, and simply, the children are saying, *We are here.* They want to speak, not just listen. They want to play, not just work. They want to perform, not just sit in the audience. They want to stand out, not fit in. They want to be teachers, not just learners. They want to be known and seen as children, not just students. They are reminding teachers to teach people, not content.

Teachers insist on moving forward in the academic content of school and the behavioral expectations of school, because—in the words of Mrs. Norbert—"we're thinking ahead to the future." They understand children to be persons-in-the-making and they are trying to make them persons who are ready for college, ready for jobs, ready for a social life of fitting in. But school shouldn't be preparation for life; for young people, *it is life*. Young people in America will spend well over a full decade of their lives in school, by law. Their daily life in school is their social and professional world—it isn't just preparation for it. They demand to matter in that world, every day.

These children are saying, *We are here now, to be seen*, for the people they already are—already full human beings, exactly as human as their teachers, no more and no less. They have things to learn as citizens, and as scholars, and as family members, and they will grow and change and develop and learn. But they are already full human beings, and none of these lessons will make them more so. They already feel and love and hurt; they already desire to be entertained and engaged and embraced; they already insist on being taken seriously and cared for deeply. They will not be ignored, and they will not be invisible.

Reflecting on the school lives of these children, recognizing the refrains in their warnings, I am reminded again of the epigraph that opens this book, from Labi Siffre's song, "Something Inside So Strong," sung each morning by children in Freedom Schools across the country: "The more you refuse to hear my voice, the louder I will sing." The more they were silenced and unseen, the more disruptively they insisted on being objects of attention.

Understanding disruption and transgression as one language children speak helps to reframe misbehavior as an expression of a set of demands—a strategy for being heard and seen. If adults were better at bearing their responsibility to see and hear children, the need for children to rely on disruption as a strategy for visibility might decrease.

The paradox of simultaneous hypervisibility and invisibility appears in the experiences of all four of these children. Zora, Lucas, Sean, and Marcus are all hypervisible as troublemakers whose names are regularly in the mouths of teachers and whose behaviors are often actively designed to draw attention. At the same time, they are invisible as human persons with complex identities beyond that of "troublemaker," as their differences are systematically erased through redirection and medication.

These children are examples of the power of disruption. They disrupt the expectation of conformity, boldly and brazenly wearing their difference and their creativity. They disrupt the demand for compliance, questioning and challenging and negotiating authority. They disrupt the requirement for quiet and stillness, fiercely insisting on their right to be both seen and heard. And they disrupt too-narrow definitions of what it means to be good, leveraging their assigned identities as troublemakers in the fight for permission to forge identities of their own choosing.

The interplay between hypervisibility and invisibility in each child's story reminds us, simply, of the power of and promise of *visibility*—of making one another fully seen and recognized, heard, valued, cherished, and protected.

As Maya Angelou reminds us, the caged bird will always sing of freedom. From their precarious perches at the entrance of the school mine, these four children not only alert us to danger, but urge us toward freedom. They urge us toward a conception of community in which power is shared, and in which there are no throwaway lives. None are sacrificed to serve the needs of others. They make *human being* visible, recentering the fundamental needs and rights of the person: to be understood, to be loved, to be powerful.

A *Letter to Teachers*

On Teaching Love and Learning Freedom

To our dear teachers:

Like you, I have a lot of books for teachers collecting dust on my shelves. The overwhelming majority of these books are packed with things to *do*—advice from "experts." They include hundreds of lists of tips, strategies, surefire, no-fail techniques for everything from teaching a child to read to getting a rowdy class to settle down.

Each time I met a child with behaviors that challenged me, I bought a classroom management book. I was convinced that one of those thousands of tips would be the silver bullet I needed. But I have now spent more than a decade reading all kinds of classroom management books—old and new, popular and obscure. I can tell you with confidence that this expert advice for how to deal with troublemakers has not changed in several decades. I read a book from 1964 that sounded like it could have been written yesterday by Doug Lemov.

Teacher books that tell us what to do, and exactly how to do it, are very alluring. But as our classroom management books gather dust, three-year-olds are getting suspended at higher rates than ever before. Youth jails are proliferating, filled with the students we push out of our classrooms. Schools that cannot afford a nurse or a social worker spend their limited funds on police and metal detectors. These books about what to *do* with our troublemakers fail us.

In part, they miss the mark because classroom management is not a technical or a mechanical skill; it is deeply relational, human work. How we manage our authority in a classroom is rife with questions of power. Our everyday interactions in classrooms are layered with histories, perspectives, identities. And how we treat our troublemakers is a question of freedom.

So this cannot be a book about what to do. I can only offer ideas about how to be. And I propose that we *be love*. Up to this point, I have argued against a set of practices that result in a pervasive culture of throwaway lives. I have talked about things going wrong. Now I want to argue for a set of practices that might move us toward a pervasive culture of freedom. I want to imagine what things could look like if they were going (more) right.

If you be love, as a teacher, then what you model is the belief—through the everyday things you do—that no human being deserves to suffer any threat to or assault on her personhood. It means that even in the face of a young person constantly calling out, cursing you out, or throwing a chair, you be love in a response that disciplines rather than punishes. You be love by modeling healing over harm. You be love by restoring community instead of excluding from community.

People misunderstand the meaning of love in public life. On the surface it can seem easy to be love. We can be less mean, more forgiving. We can yell less and smile more. Public love is confused with things like affection, kindness, politeness. I am talking instead about a love that is fierce, powerful, political, insistent. This kind of love is not easy. Authentic public love necessarily demands conflict, tears, and hurt, because our transition to freedom and to more human ways of being requires that we call ourselves out in order to call others in.[18] It requires that we be willing to confront one another, and that we be willing to listen generously when we are being confronted—letting go of our personal feelings for a commitment, instead, to the shared goal of freedom. Can we imagine our classrooms as a place to practice these revolutionary ways of being? If being love means materially changing the conditions of our world, we can begin to understand why it is hard work. And it becomes clear that we need to start practicing early, as young children, with the support of adults who are teaching and learning alongside us.

I don't know what this public love will look like in every classroom moment. Problems of freedom in classrooms are thorny and complex, and we won't always know what to do. But teachers can ask, in those moments when they are unsure, what they could *do* to *be* love. How will you be love when you choose what to hang on your walls and how to arrange your desks? How will you be love when students who cannot afford lunch are watching you eat your snack? How will you be love when your colleagues tell you to lock your purse up in the morning because the students might steal from you? How will you be love when one child hits another?

We can be regular in the way we treat troublemakers, or we can be love. The regular way is familiar to us; it's what we see, it's how we were trained, and its normalcy pulses through our minds and classrooms. It looks something like this:

The Regular Way
1. Determine and post classroom rules and norms.
2. Use systems of rewards and punishments to enforce rules and norms.
3. Flag individuals who consistently violate the rules and norms.
4. Intervene on these individuals and their behaviors by punishing and/or pathologizing.
5. Exclude individuals who ultimately cannot or will not adhere to rules and norms.

Things we might do, if we are being regular, include pulling children out into the hallway, sending them to the principal's office, isolating their desks, threatening to call their parents, recommending evaluations, and other efforts to force and scare them into new ways of being. We often think these ways "work" because, ultimately, they result in us getting rid of the problem (and, often, getting rid of the child herself). But what have we taught, in this approach, about the rights and responsibilities of freedom? Isolating and excluding young people—the regular way—is most useful if you are preparing them for our prison culture. Prison culture demands and relies on this kind of teaching.

If you are preparing young people for freedom, then community is a better place for discipline than solitary confinement. It's hard to learn freedom from inside a cage. Being love means practicing the skills required by community, *in community*.

I am convinced that if we continue to prepare children for the world we have now, we will necessarily reflect and reinforce the everyday harms and assaults of punishment, confinement, and exclusion. Instead, we have to begin to prepare children for the world we want. In schools where teachers feel stuck in how to break the harmful patterns of their classroom management, I often wonder if we might become unstuck by first imagining a world in which police are not necessary, in which prisons are abolished. What are the skills required for *that* world—skills demanded by the need to keep one another safe and free—and how might we teach and learn those skills in school as our approach to classroom management?

Being love is unfamiliar and uncomfortable. It requires an act of imagination, a leap of faith, and an extraordinary degree of hard work. It is difficult to build classrooms in the image of a freedom that we have not yet authentically seen in the world. But here we can take a cue from children, especially the youngest ones, who are masters of imagination. Their ideas are not yet impeded by reality. Consider the following exchange in a first-grade classroom:

Teacher: Let's guess the hidden word! "Jose's cat likes to drink
m_____."

Student 1: Mouse!

Teacher: Let's see if that makes sense. Cats eat mice; they
don't drink them.

Student 2: Well, if a cat kills a mouse it can drink its blood.

Student 3: Yeah! And if you put a mouse in a blender, you
could make a mouse milk shake. And the cat could drink
the mouse milk shake.

Can we adults manage to emulate this kind of audacious imagination, this refusal and inability to just fill in the blank as expected? Might we be willing to imagine our classrooms as free, beautiful places that don't yet exist in the outside world?

The young people will be experts in the imagination this work requires. I am not the expert. All I can offer here is a start, a way to move us toward being able to leverage the creative expertise of children and young people in classrooms. Toward that end, I propose a contrast to the regular way:

The Regular Way	Toward a Loving Way
1. Determine and post classroom rules and norms.	1. Discuss the meaning of freedom, and the rights and responsibilities of free people.
2. Use systems of reward and punishment to enforce rules and norms.	2. Present problems of freedom that are common in classroom life, and practice how we might respond when they happen.
3. Flag individuals who consistently violate the rules and norms.	3. Notice behaviors that pose a potential threat to freedom.

(*continued on next page*)

The Regular Way	Toward a Loving Way
4. Intervene on these individuals and their behaviors by punishing and/or pathologizing.	4. Bring these observations to the classroom community, and model and facilitate a curious approach to what they may be signaling. *The kind of questions you might ask include:* • Is there a kind of suffering that might show itself in behaviors like this? • Are there things people need that they aren't getting in our classroom? • What kinds of feelings might be behind these behaviors?
5. Exclude individuals who ultimately cannot or will not adhere to rules and norms.	5. Identify a human need that the behavior may be signaling, and decide together on a way you will all try to meet it. Revisit, over time, whether this attempt has been successful. Are people suffering less?

Building on these new modes of being, ask children to wonder, alongside you, how this human need might reflect a problem of freedom out in the world. Consider what you might teach and learn in order to intervene on those larger social problems.

To imagine how *being love* might play out, we can take Marcus as an example. Marcus invested himself in a range of challenging behaviors, from ignoring the teacher's directives to throwing a chair. Most teachers in most schools would have suspended him repeatedly. He attended a uniquely compassionate school that worked extraordinarily hard to avoid that particular form of exclusion. Despite the fact that he was never physically removed from school, however, he was marginalized and isolated in other ways in response to his behaviors. He was positioned as constantly "in trouble," by way of repeated redirection, lengthy stints in the take-a-break area of the classroom, visits to the psychologist, social worker, and principal's office, frequent trips to the class next door for time-outs. All the kids knew he was "bad," and this served as a form of exclusion from the community, despite the school's refusal to suspend him.

Marcus received an array of supports designed to help him, from very well-meaning and caring adults. But these were individual, psychological interventions that assumed only Marcus needed help, instead of assuming that Marcus was helping us to see some harm. They were the regular way. He never responded positively to these supports. And thus, despite a well-intentioned and compassionate school response, overall, he remained headed toward trouble and badness and confinement, rather than healing and goodness and freedom.

If we imagine, instead, a way to be love with Marcus, we start with tapping the expertise of children. You will need their help because they understand one another better than adults understand them. None of us remembers what it feels like to be six years old.

We can start with a question that moves us toward curiosity and away from evaluation:

Is there a harm this child is suffering to which this behavior might be a response? What if we were to gather all the kids for a public conversation—instead of pulling the troublemaker out for a private conversation—and call out the unacceptable behaviors we are witnessing with the goal in mind of calling in some responses that invite curiosity, understanding, forgiveness, transformation? The point isn't to arrive at a clear answer about what to do. The point is to model a response to troublemakers that values inclusion over exclusion and that understands behavior as a social problem rather than just an individual one. So we might simply say, "Usually people behave in certain ways to meet a human need. They could be responding to something going wrong in the way we're treating one another. But I need help figuring out what the need is, and what's going wrong. We can't have a classroom where people are suffering."

Then we can move to a question that places the needs of individuals in a shared, social context:

Can we wonder, together, how the problem we are seeing in our classroom might be related to a problem that we see out in the world? Ultimately, Marcus was understood to have anger problems. He was medicated in response to the notion that he needed help with anger management. Considering his behavior as a political problem— rather than thinking in terms of a psychological diagnosis—allows us to be curious about how anger might be a response to a problem of power rather than a lack of self-control in the individual.

So in this case we might say, "Some of us seem to be feeling angry. I'm not sure, but that's what it seems like. Are there things happening that are making some of you feel angry, even if you're not showing your anger in the same ways? Am I wrong that what I'm seeing is anger? Is it some other kind of feeling that just looks like anger?"

For Marcus, I wondered if what looked like anger was actually deep fear. I considered Marcus carefully, lovingly, as a young black boy in a world where people who look like him are so regularly understood as bad—even dangerous—almost automatically. This wasn't abstract in his witness; it concretely materialized in his weekly visits to see his father in prison. He saw a man whom he knew to be good, treated as bad, excluded from the community of goodness—removed, isolated, punished, thrown away.

For a child such as Marcus, a young black boy, being seen as good is not just a psychological preference. It is a requirement for survival in a country where twelve-year-olds who look like him are shot dead by police for being tall for their age, and seventeen-year-olds who look like him are shot dead by overzealous neighborhood watchmen for buying candy at night.

Is it not reasonable for Marcus to feel angry? Is it not reasonable for him to understand how important it is, to his survival, to be seen as good?

What would it look like—and what would it signal—if we used school as a place to invite young people to understand problems of power together, to recognize hurt and anger as righteous, as sensible responses to the world in which we live? What would it mean if we mobilized young people to address these human harms, practicing first in the relative safety of our classrooms, so they could then graduate to thoughtfully, fiercely, intelligently, bravely addressing human harms in the world beyond school?

These would be ways to teach love. To learn freedom, we would then need to ask:

How will we try to heal one another, to address human needs, and to alleviate harms to human being that we see out in the world? The late activist and philosopher Grace Lee Boggs taught us the need to raise children and to encourage adults to be "solutionaries," revolutionary problem solvers with audacious imagination. How to address the injustices that plague us—the poisons that trigger the suffering of our children—is a question for the children to take up, with our facilitation and our honest admission that we don't have the answers. No single one of us has the creativity, the courage, or the skill enough to teach love and learn freedom alone. This is work that requires an imagination developed together, the courage of a community, and the combined skills of each member of that community. I say this with the utmost love, reverence, and respect for you as a teacher: you aren't the expert. So gather your humility, forget everything you learned about how teachers are supposed to know everything, and begin to learn freedom from your students.

These are difficult and beautiful times to be a teacher. For some of us, the horror of mass shootings and bombings shock us into feelings of renewed urgency in our work. For others—those who teach children for whom terror, trauma, and toxic stress are everyday rather than episodic—the urgency is constant, numbing in its assault. We can all feel beaten down, exhausted, and hopeless. These are times to remember our power as teachers. In no other profession do people have the opportunity to literally create a parallel world—a world that is safer, fairer, freer. The four walls of your classroom can be the world we want, hope for, dream of, rather than the world we have now. It can allow children to practice the skills they need to create and to sustain a place where people are neither shunned nor labeled; a shared, public place in which every community member is treated as a free person, an invaluable person, a gifted and good and loved person.

Responding differently to our troublemakers is paramount to meeting our responsibilities as educators and as human beings. What we call "classroom management" is an assault on freedom. Points, rewards, threats, treats, traffic-light systems, demerits, and detentions are used by the person in power to police the boundaries of acceptable behavior. A young person's place in the community is thus conditional—contingent upon his ability and willingness to stay within the policed boundaries. If you are too disruptive, you lose your place in the community.

How stressful it must be to be a young person in our schools! How unsafe and frightening it must be to wonder—as you witness the punishment and rejection of one of your peers—if you will be next. That kind of conditional acceptance, subjective belonging, contingent care, must feel terribly threatening to children, whom we know are biologically wired to make illogical choices as their brains continue to develop. They make mistakes and they make bad decisions—don't we all? Especially when we are stressed, feeling unsafe, and suffering?

We need new ideas about what it means to make our schools safe. If we are awake in this political moment, we know that police are not a resource for making us safe—especially if we are not white. Safe schools don't have police; they have love. Human beings feel safe when they know their personhood will not be assaulted by way of marginalization, public humiliation, and rejection. They feel safe when they are accepted, embraced, cherished—even when they mess up. Police can't be responsible for providing this kind of safety. It isn't in their job description. This is a task of education and it falls on our shoulders as teachers.

We need schools in which children and adults are teaching one another the skills that a free world will require: how to listen and how to speak, in our own languages and in one another's languages; how to read, broadly defined; how to heal and be healed; how to use numbers to understand problems and measure our own solutions; how to be love.

Teachers are on the front lines of making things more right. You are the holders of our precious communities of children—their caretakers, their advocates, their teachers. We adults are going to one day leave this world to the children sitting in your classrooms. They will be tasked with caring for the babies, the elders, the ailing planet. We need them to do a better job than we have. Let's start by offering them a solid model of how to teach love, so we might all finally begin to learn freedom.

Love,

Carla

A Note to All Readers

On Mushrooms, Mold, and Mice

I am writing from our home in Detroit. I have found this city—the most racially segregated in the nation, and arguably the most depressed by policies that ensure extreme poverty—to be an extraordinary place to consider how people teach love and learn freedom. Both abandoned by corporations and actively harmed by government officials, poor people in Detroit have had to provide one another with their own goods and services. In an effort at survival, they turn abandoned lots into urban gardens in order to feed their blocks. They literally put their bodies in the way of moving trucks hired to remove their neighbors' belongings from foreclosed homes. Everyday people engineer makeshift street lamps that work on solar energy. The elders teach the young people to make rain barrels and mobile water filtration systems as a solution to massive water shutoffs perpetrated by those who believe natural resources are for selling, buying, and selectively withholding.

Detroit is a place to learn freedom because people here have already learned that elected officials cannot be trusted to take care of them. They're striving to remember that "opportunity is created by crisis," as Grace Lee Boggs always told us, and they're working to enact their own government by the people, for the people, out of sheer necessity. We can learn from Detroit as we continue to mourn the election of a United States president who promises to make life even more difficult and dangerous for communities of color, by learning to *be love* in the face of hateful and active neglect, turning to one another for protection and for solutions. We can teach ourselves, and our children, to be the *solutionaries* Grace Lee Boggs imagined, and to create the world anew.

So I want to close the book by bringing you all here to Detroit and, specifically, to our schools. If you want to know the true health of a nation, I always think you ought to look inside its schools. And here, we might all learn something from Detroit's teachers.

In the state of Michigan, by law, teachers are not allowed to strike. But I have written about free people, and about how free people break rules when their dignity demands it and when their warnings are urgent enough to require it. In 2016, the teachers in our city temporarily closed down ninety of our ninety-five public schools by calling out sick, en masse, to protest the poisonous conditions of their schools—schools where mushrooms, mold, and mice thrive in the buildings, while young people cannot.

These teachers are forbidden to take photographs of the conditions in their schools. They are required to keep these poisons private, secret, invisible. But they decided instead to make them public, hypervisible on social and other media. They united in a community of refusal despite the risks. They broke the rules. Troublemakers. And now all the world can see into these classrooms where ceilings chip and fall, toilets leak sewage, and old furnaces in desperate need of maintenance threaten to erupt into flames.

Administrators within the Detroit public school system, along with a solid cohort of lawmakers in the state of Michigan, are seeking ways to punish the teachers for their actions. They want to rescind the teaching certification of those who participated in the protests, and to hold hearings that punish protestors for breaking the spirit of the law that prohibits teacher strikes. These miseducated leaders—who likely did very well in school—failed to learn the responsibilities, the demands, of freedom. I am struck by the seemingly irresistible temptation to punish the troublemakers instead of heeding their warnings, hearing their cries. How familiar, resonant, and predictable a response.

The images of these Detroit classrooms are enough to make anyone sick. Inside school buildings, black and gray mushrooms multiply and spread, climbing the walls like poisonous ivy. Green, yellow, and orange molds grow on floors, around desks and chairs. Cabinets and drawers and room corners are littered with mouse feces. The conditions are toxic.

I have been writing metaphorically, up to this point, about harmful poisons in the air of our schools and about dehumanizing conditions. Now I am speaking literally. These schools, where mushrooms, mold, and mice thrive, are toxic to human beings. We send our children—our babies, our most precious young people— into these school buildings day after day. That this is allowed to go on—that children are in fact required by law to attend these schools—is perhaps the clearest and most concrete evidence I can offer of our collective national commitment to throwaway lives, particularly the lives of poor, young people of color. A first grader is sitting in a classroom with mice, breathing mold into her young, fragile lungs. Why is the whole nation not up in arms?

I have now said repeatedly that free people are those who can recognize when they, and others, are being treated as less than fully human. Free persons embrace both their right and their duty to struggle against such treatment and to organize with others in a solidary community of refusal. Our ability to *not* care about the daily assaults to the personhood of children and teachers in Detroit reveals that we are not free persons. We are, instead, a nation committed to the insistence that only some lives matter.

Looking at photos of the classrooms in Detroit makes this commitment to throwaway lives painfully visible. We can *see* the mushrooms, mold, and mice. Though these are literally poisonous to the health of human beings, they are really only the surface symptoms of more insidious diseases. That is to say, we could exterminate the mushrooms, mold, and mice, but the roots that give rise to them in the first place will simply reproduce them—again and again.

So we need to dig deeper, and to be more radical (at the root) in our approach to identifying the harms our children breathe daily. In this case, if we want to identify the original disease, the one at the root of these more visible symptoms, we might ask: *Why are there no mushrooms, mold, or mice where wealthy white children go to school?*

It is not enough to build new schools for the young people of Detroit, schools free of poison. Instead, freedom demands a collective effort to engage the young people of Detroit in building a new world, for themselves and for us, in which we do not permit human beings to be poisoned in the first place. The imagination for such an effort begins with the model their teachers provide in their refusal to keep the assaults on their students invisible. They have chosen to reject private suffering in favor of public pedagogy.

Their lessons have resonated. One of our city's tenth graders, Imani Harris, published a widely shared letter putting her freedom learning on display.[19] She wrote:

I know my rights, and I know that the color of my skin does NOT give anyone the right to give me any different of an education than a white girl would get. . . . Everyone's so worried about how I'm losing my education from four sickout days. No one's taking into account the fact that I went almost a full semester without a real English teacher. Let's count up those days and see just how much education I missed from those MONTHS, while the powers that be took their sweet time finding a teacher that was actually willing to step foot into DPS due to the instability and lack of value of teachers by this state run district.

These teachers *be* love by loudly saying enough is enough. Their students are learning from their model. They are part of a movement here in Detroit to enact visionary resistance in response to the state-sanctioned assaults on young people, their schools, and their communities. They are heeding the call of Charity Hicks, an activist in our city who struggled fiercely against water shutoffs, to "wage love"—to resist, to transform, and to refuse assaults on the rights of people to be free. We are seeing this more and more—teachers waging love, making public their efforts to teach love and to learn freedom through protests that bring national attention to local assaults on young human beings in school. These teachers are on strike in Seattle and in New York and in Chicago, refusing to let their schools be closed and refusing to give so many tests to children and refusing to let the police kill their students with impunity.

The visible activism of organized educators in cities across the country is an invitation to all of us—educators and non-educators alike—to participate in their lessons. The problems to which they draw our attention, the multitude of manifestations of mushrooms, mold, and mice thriving in our nation's schools, are an urgent call to action. I have argued that young troublemakers are the people from whom we can learn the most about freedom, if only we could succeed in refusing to cage them. And that troublemaking teachers must come out of their isolated classrooms to find one another out on the streets, making public the lessons they've learned in solidarity with young people. We need all raise our hands to participate in these lessons. We need all raise our voices in fierce resistance to throwaway lives, so the burden to sing freedom does not rest alone on the shoulders of our children.

Acknowledgments

To the four children featured in this book—for your creativity, your brilliance, and most of all, your goodness—I thank you. May you always make trouble if your freedom demands it. And to the families, teachers, and principals who welcomed me into the world of these children—for your trust, patience, and extraordinary generosity—I thank you.

To my own first and best teachers:
My sister, Dalia Mirrione—for teaching me to read and to write, and for walking ahead to leave all those doors open for me—I thank you and I love you. I became a teacher because of you.

My mama—for teaching me to love and to fight, and for crying over the pain of strangers so that I learned the empathy required to treat all children as if they were my own—I thank you and I love you. I became more human because of you.

My dad—for teaching me the meaning of hard work, and for being so proud of me that you spent much of my childhood behind a camera lens trying to record every shining moment—I thank you and I love you. I became a writer because of you.

To Sophia, my niece—while writing this book, I often thought about the day you were born. Seeing you for the first time and holding you as a tiny baby reminded me how precious and fragile our babies are, and how much responsibility we have to carefully protect you. I will always have your back, my love.

To Jordan, my incredible YouTube video–making nephew—you are too special and extraordinary to fit in everywhere, so I hope you never worry too much about fitting in and, like Zora in this book, insist on your right to be *out-standing*.

And to Trevor, my zany, hilarious, tech-savvy nephew—you are a genius. I think you are so smart and that your ideas are so good. Maybe school doesn't always make you feel that way, but I know the truth about your brilliant brain and this book is supposed to help teachers know the truth about kids, too.

To my aunt Mimi and my uncle Salah, for being my second parents, I thank you and I love you. To my cousin Emil, who insisted on my smarts (and often takes credit for them), and his sister, Nancy, a fierce example of strong womanhood and the only person who read my dissertation by choice, I thank you and I love you.

To the intellectual giants who offered me shoulders to stand on:
Sara Lawrence-Lightfoot—for valuing both distance and intimacy in scholarship, for modeling both rigor and accessibility, for celebrating both art and science, for encouraging both theory and practice, I thank you. Your own commitment to recognizing and documenting goodness—in beautiful form—has been deeply inspiring and critically instructive.

Wendy Luttrell—for teaching me the power and the possibilities of art as a tool for making the unseen *seen*, recognized, and resurrected, I thank you. You always shared and bolstered my belief in the particular brilliance of young children, and my curiosity in how they see. You are a rare, beautiful, and steadfast example of what it means to be human in the academy.

Jim Giarelli—for being my first teacher in critical theory, for centering ethics, for modeling the generous balance of the humor and seriousness required in school and in life, I thank you. I once came to you, downtrodden, having been to the library and noticed that every book I had ever wanted to write was already written. You said that nobody had written a book in the particular way that I would. (I hope you're right.)

Thea Abu El-Haj—for fundamentally transforming my understanding of *difference* by teaching me to question things taken for granted as normal, for offering me an intellectual and cultural space of home at Rutgers, and for teaching me the interconnectedness of struggle and our place in it as Arabs and Arab-Americans, I thank you.

Dirck Roosevelt—for gently correcting my many moments of overstepping the narrative voice, for consistently reminding me to check my own interpretations in favor of the meanings children offered, and for helping me take a close, careful, *good* look at each of these four children, I thank you.

To my lifelong sister-friends—Rupal Parekh and Janine Keil Garcia, Cari Mae Johnson Lopez and Andrea Kecskes Gingras, Angela Razzano, Laura Lebo, Laura Williamson Ambrose, and Nisha Aidasani—for being my chosen family, my steadfast cheerleaders, and for all the love and laughter through thick and thin, I thank you and I love you. Rupal, I particularly thank you for your marketing genius in helping me think about the best ways to help ideas reach people.

To my invaluable writing group—Keith Catone and Thomas Nikundiwe—for being the best possible allies in the work, in the word, and in the world, I thank you. You are fierce and generous critics, and I love how proud we are of each other.

To my students—at Brooks Crossing Elementary, Rutgers, Brown, Wellesley, and Michigan State—for teaching me more about teaching than I ever thought possible, I thank you. I wish I could name each of you. You'll hear yourselves, and our work together, in the pages of this book.

To my earliest teacher colleagues—my mentor teacher, Allie Cavaliere Hart; and the original fourth- and fifth-grade team at Brooks Crossing, including Lorraine Bagley, Barb Bowen Capasso, Neel Desai, Glenn Ferraris, Christie Hardy, Melissa Heath, Debi LiMato, Joe Mersinger, Mirna Roney, Tracey Ricco, and Amanda Rapp Smith—I thank you all for having my back when I was targeted for being too much of a troublemaker.

To my HGSE comrades—Gretchen Brion-Meisels, Sherry Deckman, Jen Dorsey, Chantal Francois, Julia Galindo, Soo Hong, Irene Liefshitz, Meredith Mira, Santiago Rincon-Gallardo, Kenneth Russell, Sola Takahashi, Mandy Taylor, Anita Wadhwa, and Ming Wang—for making it all somehow livable, I thank you! To Karen Mapp and Donal Fox—for giving me a place to (literally) call home while writing my dissertation—I thank you. Boston winters were made warm by your care. And to Wendy Angus—for your invaluable support, patience, and help at each and every stop along this journey—I thank you.

To my incredible and committed editors, I thank you. Tara Grove advocated, understood, and patiently navigated both my stubbornness as a human being and my naïveté as a first-time author. Ellen Adler told me the truth, insisted when it mattered, and helped me push through a title and cover art that are responsible, accurate, and lovely. And to the generous humans who voluntarily read earlier drafts of chapters to help me think through difficult things—Leigh Patel, who offers necessary critique in a way that feels like love; and Margaret Kavanagh, who loves by giving lots of necessary critique—I thank you both so, so much. No doubt this work was made smarter and more beautiful because of the lenses these four particular women brought.

To the colleagues and friends new and old who supported this work through conversations formal and informal, over coffee and through texts and in all the breakdown moments, I thank you—Jason Moore, Dulari Tahbildar, and Brian Hayes. And to those who helped usher me through graduate school and the start of my career beyond Harvard by giving me my first chances, I thank you—Deborah Ball, Prudence Carter, John Diamond, Mica Pollock, and Mark Warren.

To my partner, in love and in life, in the work and in the world, Thomas Nikundiwe—for teaching me to create a *we* powerful and loving enough to do the work this world needs, starting at home, I thank you. Your lessons in listening teach me to hear young voices with curiosity, with love, and with reverence. This book could never have happened without you, and every word and sentence echoes with lessons I've learned from *we*. You make me smarter and stronger.

And, finally, to the feisty, bold, literally wonder-full children who fuel my work and who give my days meaning—I thank you. To Izaac, a tremendously gifted, brilliant, and exceptional young man for whom school will never work, I love you for so often being the only person who truly understands how I'm feeling, and for inspiring this book in the first place. And to Akenna, a little firecracker of energy with perfect comedic timing, who teaches me that fun is the lifeblood of children and play is the heart of their learning, I adore you because of (and despite) your troublemaking antics.

Suggested Resources

Recommended Reading

The Boy Who Was Raised as a Dog, and Other Stories from a Child Psychiatrist's Notebook: What Traumatized Children Can Teach Us About Loss, Love, and Healing by Bruce Perry

Calling the Circle: The First and Future Culture by Christina Baldwin

The Compassionate Classroom: Relationship Based Teaching and Learning by Sura Hart and Victoria Kindle Hodson

Educating for Insurgency: The Roles of Young People in Schools of Poverty by Jay Gillen

Far from the Tree: Parents, Children, and the Search for Identity by Andrew Solomon

Hope and Healing in Urban Education: How Urban Activists and Teachers Are Reclaiming Matters of the Heart by Shawn Ginwright

Justice as Healing: Writings on Community Peacemaking and Restorative Justice from the Native Law Centre by Wanda McCaslin

The Little Book of Restorative Justice by Howard Zehr

The New Jim Crow: Mass Incarceration in the Age of Colorblindness by Michelle Alexander

Nonviolent Communication: A Language of Life by Marshall B. Rosenberg

Octavia's Brood: Science Fiction Stories from Social Justice Movements, edited by Walidah Imarisha, adrienne maree brown, and Sheree Renee Thomas

Peacemaking Circles and Urban Youth: Bringing Justice Home by Carolyn Boyes-Watson

Pedagogy of Freedom: Ethics, Democracy, and Civic Courage by Paulo Freire

Pedagogy of the Oppressed by Paulo Freire

The Pedagogy of Teacher Activism: Portraits of Four Teachers for Justice by Keith Catone

Pushout: The Criminalization of Black Girls in Schools by Monique Morris

Restorative Justice in Urban Schools: Disrupting the School-to-Prison Pipeline by Anita Wadhwa

Teaching Children Compassionately: How Students and Teachers Can Succeed with Mutual Understanding by Marshall B. Rosenberg

Zero Tolerance: Resisting the Drive for Punishment in our Schools: A Handbook for Parents, Students, Educators, and Citizens by William Ayers, Rick Ayers, and Bernardine Dohrn (editors)

Teaching Resources and Relevant Social Justice Organizations

Advancement Project—*Ending the Schoolhouse to Jailhouse* track is one program of the Advancement Project, a next-generation, multi-racial civil rights organization. The site is full of information, teaching materials, and other resources for students, parents, educators, law enforcement, and activists. (safequalityschools.org)

Centre for Justice and Reconciliation: A program of Prison Fellowship International—an organization whose mission is to develop and promote restorative justice in criminal justice systems around the world. The site includes a useful RJ library full of additional resources. (restorativejustice .org/rj-library)

Critical Resistance—an organization committed to building an "international movement to end the prison industrial complex by challenging the belief that caging and controlling people makes us safe." (criticalresistance.org)

Detroit Future Schools—an organization that places teaching artists in public schools to partner with teachers in critical pedagogy media projects. They publish a Guide to Humanizing Schooling that details their root practices and principles. (detroitfutureschools.org)

Dignity in Schools Campaign—an organization that "challenges the systemic problem of pushout in our nation's schools and works to dismantle the school-to-prison pipeline." (dignityinschools.org)

Education for Liberation Network—a national coalition of teachers, community activists, researchers, youth, and parents who believe that a good education should teach people—particularly low-income youth and youth of color—how to understand and challenge the injustices their communities face. (edliberation.org)

IndyKids! A Free Paper for Free Kids—a progressive current-events newspaper and teacher's guide for kids grades four through seven. (indykids.org)

Picturing a World Without Prisons—a photography project that begins the process of visualizing prison abolition and transformative justice (cargocollective .com/worldwithoutprisons)

Planning to Change the World: A Plan Book for Social Justice Teachers—a planner for educators who believe their students can and will change the world, designed to help teachers translate their vision of a just education into concrete classroom activities. The plan book is updated and published annually. (justiceplanbook.com)

Project NIA—a grassroots advocacy, organizing, popular education, research, and capacity-building center with the long-term goal of ending youth incarceration. The website includes a wealth of tools and resources about restorative and transformative justice, and their own recommended book list. (project-nia.org)

Project SOUTH—a Southern-based leadership development organization that uses four major strategies to build political, educational, and economic power at the grassroots of low-income communities: popular education, leadership development, partnerships and alliances, and organizing. The organization provides toolkits and curriculum resources for educators and organizers. (projectsouth.org)

Responsive Classroom—an approach to teaching that emphasizes academic, social, and emotional growth in a strong school community. (responsiveclass room.org)

Restorative Posters: Representing Justice Visually—free, downloadable posters that center the tenets of restorative justice. (rjposters.com)

Rethinking Schools—an activist publication with articles written for and by teachers, parents, and students. Teachers can subscribe to the magazine and/ or see their list of books for educators. (rethinkingschools.org)

Safe Schools Coalition—a public-private partnership in support of gay, lesbian, bisexual, and transgender queer and questioning youth. (safeschools coalition.org)

Sentencing Project—working for a fair and effective U.S. criminal justice system. The website includes a page specifically devoted to juvenile justice that includes key publications of relevance to those working with young people. (sentencingproject.org)

Teaching for Change: Building Social Justice Starting in the Classroom— provides teachers and parents with the tools to create schools where teachers and students question and rethink the world inside and outside their classrooms, build a more equitable, multicultural society, and become active global citizens. The website includes many rich teaching resources and curriculum materials by theme and age group, as well as vetted children and young adult book lists. (teachingforchange.org)

Teaching Tolerance—a project of the South Poverty Law Center, Teaching Tolerance is a place for educators who care about diversity, equity, and justice, and can find news, suggestions, conversation, support, and rich curricular materials organized by topic and age level. (tolerance.org)

YES! magazine—a free publication that inspires educators to shape a more just and sustainable future with stories of positive solutions. (yesmagazine .org)

Zinn Education Project—promotes and supports the teaching of people's history in middle and high school classrooms across the country. (zinnedproject .org)

Teacher Activist Groups

Association of Raza Educators (Los Angeles)—razaeducators.org
Educators Network for Social Justice (Milwaukee)—ensj.weebly.org
Educators for Social Justice (St. Louis)—www.educatorsforsocialjustice.org
Metro Atlantans for Public Schools (Atlanta)—map.school.wikispaces.com
New York Collective of Radical Educators (NYCoRE)—nycore.org
People's Education Movement (Los Angeles and the Bay Area)—
    peoplesed.org
Teacher Action Group (Boston)—tagboston.org
Teacher Action Group (Philadelphia)—tagphilly.org
Teacher Activist Groups (TAG, a national coalition)—
    teacheractivistgroups.org
Teachers for Social Justice (Chicago)—teachersforjustice.org
Teachers 4 Social Justice (San Francisco)—t4sj.org

Conferences and Gatherings

Allied Media Conference—alliedmedia.org/amc

Creating Balance in an Unjust World: Math Education and Social Justice—creatingbalanceconference.org

Creating Change Conference, National LGBTQ Task Force—creatingchange.org

Free Minds Free People—fmfp.org

Liberation Healing Conference—facebook.com/liberationbasedhealingconferences

New York Collective of Radical Educators conference—nycore.org/conference/nycore-conference

Northwest Conference on Teaching for Social Justice—nwtsj.org

Teachers 4 Social Justice Conference—t4sj.org

Notes

1. U.S. Department of Education, Office for Civil Rights, "2013–2014 Civil Rights Data Collection: A First Look," June 7, 2016, www2.ed.gov /about/offices/list/ocr/docs/2013-14-first-look.pdf.

2. This father credited his own uptake of this analogy to a book by Lani Guinier and Gerald Torres entitled *The Miner's Canary: Enlisting Race, Resisting Power, Transforming Democracy* (Cambridge, MA: Harvard University Press, 2003), in which the authors argue that "those who are racially marginalized are the miner's canary: their distress is the first sign of a danger that threatens us all" (11).

3. Philip Jackson, *Life in Classrooms* (New York: Holt, Rinehart and Winston, 1968).

4. Sara E. Rimm-Kaufman, Robert C. Pianta, and Martha J. Cox, "Teachers Judgments of the Problems in the Transition to Kindergarten," *Early Childhood Quarterly* 15, No. 2 (2000): 147–166.

5. Sueanne E. McKinney, Gloria D. Campbell-Whately, and Cathy D. Kea, "Managing Student Behavior in Urban Classrooms: The Role of Teacher ABC Assessments," *The Clearing House* 79, No. 1 (2005): 16–20.

6. Donald J. Hernandez, *Double Jeopardy: How Third-Grade Reading Skills and Poverty Influence High School Graduation* (Baltimore, MD: Annie E. Casey Foundation, 2012), www.aecf.org/m/resourcedoc/AECF-DoubleJeop ardy-2012-Full.pdf.

7. For a powerful and provocative explication of the similarities between life on southern plantations and life in modern-day schools of poverty, see Jay Gillen, *Educating for Insurgency: The Roles of Young People in Poverty* (Oakland, CA: AK Press, 2014). He offers a compelling explanation of the role of schools in maintaining the American racial caste system.

8. Sara Lawrence-Lightfoot and Jessica Hoffmann Davis, *The Art and Science of Portraiture* (San Francisco: Jossey-Bass, 1997).

9. Carter G. Woodson, *The Mis-Education of the Negro* (Trenton, NJ: Africa World Press, Inc., 1933), 9–10.

10. W.E.B. DuBois, *The Souls of Black Folk: Essays and Sketches* (Chicago: A.C. McClurg & Co.; Cambridge, MA: University Press John Wilson and Son, 1903), 2.

11. Jackson, *Life in Classrooms*, 30.

12. Ibid., 17.

13. Ann Arnett Ferguson, *Bad Boys: Public Schools in the Making of Black Masculinity* (Ann Arbor: University of Michigan Press, 2000), 177.

14. Ibid., 177.

15. See Cynthia B. Dillard, *Learning to (Re)member the Things We've Learned to Forget: Endarkened Feminisms, Spirituality, and the Sacred Nature of Research and Teaching* (New York: Peter Lang, 2012).

16. Jeff Duncan-Andrade, "Growing Roses in Concrete" (TED Talk, TEDxGoldenGateED, 2009).

17. The paradox of simultaneous hypervisibility and invisibility in the experiences of young people is similarly documented in several studies. See, for example, Thea Renda Abu El-Haj, "Arab Visibility and Invisibility," in *Everyday Antiracism: Getting Real About Race in School*, ed. Mica Pollock (New York: The New Press, 2008), 174–179; and see Bryan McKinley Jones Brayboy, "Hiding in the Ivy: American Indian Students and Visibility in Elite Educational Settings," *Harvard Educational Review* 74, No. 2 (2004): 125–152.

18. Ngọc Loan Trần, "Calling IN: A Less Disposable Way of Holding Each Other Accountable," *BGD Blog*, December 18, 2013, www.blackgirldangerous.org/2013/12/calling-less-disposable-way-holding-accountable.

19. "Letter from Detroit Student, Imani Harris," *The Blog, Huffington Post*, May 10, 2016, www.huffingtonpost.com/the-skillman-foundation/letter-from-detroit-student_b_9868492.html.

About the Author

Carla Shalaby is a researcher, writer, and former elementary school teacher with a professional and personal commitment to education as the practice of freedom. Her research on teaching and teacher education centers on cultivating and documenting everyday classroom work that protects the dignity of every child, honors young people's right to expression and to self-determination, and prepares learners and their teachers to take their place in the ongoing struggle for justice.

Shalaby earned her doctorate at the Harvard Graduate School of Education and has directed elementary education programs at both Brown University and Wellesley College. She co-edits an annual lesson plan book for social justice teachers, in collaboration with the Education for Liberation Network, called *Planning to Change the World*. She lives in Detroit.

Celebrating 25 Years of Independent Publishing

Thank you for reading this book published by The New Press. The New Press is a nonprofit, public interest publisher celebrating its twenty-fifth anniversary in 2017. New Press books and authors play a crucial role in sparking conversations about the key political and social issues of our day.

We hope you enjoyed this book and that you will stay in touch with The New Press. Here are a few ways to stay up to date with our books, events, and the issues we cover:

- Sign up at www.thenewpress.com/subscribe to receive updates on New Press authors and issues and to be notified about local events
- Like us on Facebook: www.facebook.com/newpressbooks
- Follow us on Twitter: www.twitter.com/thenewpress

Please consider buying New Press books for yourself; for friends and family; or to donate to schools, libraries, community centers, prison libraries, and other organizations involved with the issues our authors write about.

The New Press is a 501(c)(3) nonprofit organization. You can also support our work with a tax-deductible gift by visiting www.thenewpress.com/donate.